WIEN BEI NACHT
VIENNA BY NIGHT

WIEN BEI NACHT
VIENNA BY NIGHT

Photographien von Harry Weber

Texte von Helmut A. Gansterer

Übertragung ins Englische von Peter Waugh

Mit 225 Abbildungen in Farbe

Verlag Christian Brandstätter · Wien

1. Auflage

Die Bildauswahl und die graphische Gestaltung stammen von
Christian Brandstätter.

Das Lektorat erfolgte durch Helga Sieche, die technische Betreuung durch Rudolf Metzger.

Die Gesamtherstellung des Werkes erfolgte bei Ueberreuter in Korneuburg, gesetzt wurde in der
Walbaum, 10 auf 12 bzw. 8 auf 9 Punkt. Die Reproduktion der Farbabbildungen besorgte Reproform in Wien.

Copyright © 1992 by Christian Brandstätter Verlag, Wien
Alle Rechte, auch die des auszugsweisen Abdrucks oder der Reproduktion einer Abbildung, sind vorbehalten.
ISBN 3-85447-433-4

Christian Brandstätter Verlagsgesellschaft m. b. H.
A-1080 Wien, Wickenburggasse 26 . Telephon (0222) 408 38 14

Inhaltsverzeichnis *Contents*

WIEN NÄCHTLICH *THE NIGHT AHEAD*
Prolog *Prologue* 7
Panoramen *Panoramic Views* 10

NACHT-SCHÖNHEIT *NIGHT BEAUTIES* 17
Rund um St. Stephan *Around St. Stephen's* 18
In der Altstadt *In the Old City* 28
Rund um die Ringstraße *Around the Ringstrasse* 46
Barocke Veduten *Baroque Vedutas* 80
An der kleinen und großen Donau *The Danube* 88
Die Straßen von Wien *The Streets of Vienna* 96

NACHT-ARBEIT *NIGHT WORK* 101
Vom öffentlichen Nachtverkehr *Getting Home* 102
Vom Bauch von Wien *The Belly of Vienna* 106
Vom privaten Nachtverkehr *Not Getting Home* 112

NACHT-PLAISIR *NIGHT PLEASURE* 115
Im Café *In the Coffeehouse* 116
Beim Heurigen *At the Wine Tavern* 119
Prater *The Prater* 122
Szenelokale, Beiseln und Restaurants *Pubs, Inns and Restaurants* 128
Discos und Musiklokale *Discos and Music-Pubs* 134
Bars und Nightclubs *Bars and Nightclubs* 137
Sperrstunde *Closing Times* 140

WIEN ÜBERNÄCHTIG *THE MORNING AFTER*
Epilog *Epilogue* 141

Sperrstundenindex *Index of Closing Times* 143

Prolog *Prologue*

Es ist zehn Jahre her. Ein deutscher Journalist war zu Besuch in Wien. Ein ortskundiger Kollege führte ihn durch die Wiener Nacht. Diese spezielle Nacht war vielleicht ein wenig belebt, ein wenig vollmondig, was die Anzahl der fröhlichen Streuner betrifft. Aber *soo ungewöhnlich* war sie auch wieder nicht. Der deutsche Freund allerdings flüsterte unentwegt: „Mann, das gibt's doch nicht."

In der Armbrustergasse, beim Heurigen „Zimmermann", war ihm der große Politiker Bruno Kreisky gezeigt worden; im „Gutruf" der berühmte Mime Helmut Qualtinger, wenig später der Dramatiker Wolfi Bauer; im „Argentina" saß Formel-1-Weltstar Niki Lauda, trank einen kleinen Wodka mit; im „Oswald & Kalb" war dem deutschen Gast der André Heller ein Begriff; im „Alt-Wien" vis-à-vis scherzte Georg Danzer, in der „Bonbonniere" saß der Bürgermeister Helmut Zilk, in der „Reiss" der Weltkoch Witzigmann auf Heimaturlaub; in der „Eden" becherte ein ehemaliger Bautenminister mit dem Wirtschaftsminister, der bald darauf ein ehemaliger wurde.

Diese Versammlung außergewöhnlicher Köpfe ist tatsächlich normal, und vielleicht dramatischer als in anderen Städten. „Genies zum Angreifen" nannte das ein deutscher Publizist, Prof. Holger Rust. Der Wahlwiener hält diese Angreifbarkeit für einen wichtigen Reiz der Wiener Nacht – bis heute, obgleich die Politiker sich mittlerweile verdrückten. Nur der Bürgermeister bleibt mit tiefer Stimme tapfer auf dem Schiff. Vielleicht fürchten die Politiker die neue Verdrossenheit und den nächtlichen Schmäh des Volkes.

II.

Max Frisch schreibt einmal sinngemäß: Dummköpfe unterhalten sich über andere Menschen, Halbdumme über Vorfälle, Gescheite über Visionen.

Das ist streng. Und ein wenig unwirklich ist es auch, wenn von einer Stadt die Rede ist, der die Darsteller wichtiger als die Stücke sind. Da ist es einfach schön, wenn die Schauspielerin Susanne Widl das „Café Korb" in der Tuchlauben führt, und der Schauspieler Hanno Pöschl das „Kleine Café" am Franziskanerplatz. Claus Peymann findet man beim Solo-Dinner in den „Drei Husaren". Seinen Freund Thomas Bernhard fand man zu Lebzeiten im Café Bräunerhof. Dort las er gierig jene Literaturkritiken, „die ich grundsätzlich nicht lese".

Das Geh'n-ma-Künstler-schauen findet einen sehr menschlichen Höhepunkt im Café Hawelka. Entgegen der jahrzehntealten Sage sitzen dort *nicht immer* weltberühmte Künstler wie die Maler Pichler und Attersee oder Nobelpreisträger wie Elias Canetti. An manchen Abenden lauern dort nur kreativ gekleidete Kaffeehaustouristen und schauen einander bewundernd als Künstler an.

Schloß Schönbrunn.
Schönbrunn Palace

It was ten years ago. A German journalist was visiting Vienna. A colleague who was familiar with the city took him on a tour of the Viennese night. With regard to the number of high-spirited prowlers about, this particular night may well have been rather busy; perhaps there was a bit of a full moon. Yet it was not that unusual. Nevertheless, the German friend whispered incessantly: "Man, this is incredible!"

At the Zimmermann wine tavern in Armbrustergasse, the great politician Bruno Kreisky was pointed out to him; in Gutruf the famous Helmut Qualtinger, and a little later the dramatist Wolfgang Bauer; in Argentina sat the world star of formula 1, Niki Lauda, drinking a small vodka; in Oswald & Kalb the German visitor recognised André Heller; in Alt Wien Georg Danzer was there joking opposite them, in Bonbonniere sat the Mayor, Helmut Zilk, while in Reiss there was Witzigmann, the world-famous chef, who was taking a holiday at home; in Eden a former Minister for Building was drinking with the Minister for Trade, who became an ex-minister himself soon afterwards.

In actual fact, this assembly of interesting faces is quite normal here, and perhaps more dramatic than in other cities. The German publicist, Prof. Holger Rust, called it "geniuses within arm's reach". Those who have settled in Vienna by choice, and love it, regard this proximity as an important attraction of the Viennese night – even today, although the politicians have in the meantime made themselves scarce. Only the deep-voiced Mayor still remains bravely on board ship. Perhaps the politicians are afraid of the new moroseness and the people's nocturnal Schmäh, or playful kidding.

II.

Max Frisch writes (approximately) that: idiots talk about other people, half-idiots about events, clever people about visions.

That is hard. And it is also a little unreal, when talking about a city where the actors are more important than the play. It is just nice to have the actress Susanne Wildl as the proprietor of Café Korb *in the Tuchlauben, and the actor Hanno Pöschl as the owner of* Kleines Café *in Franziskanerplatz. Claus Peymann can be found dining alone in the* Drei Husaren. *His friend Thomas Bernhard used to be found, while he was still alive, in Café Bräunerhof. There he greedily read the literary reviews "which I don't read as a matter of principle".*

The 'let's go look at some artists' situation reaches a very human peak in Café Hawelka. Despite the stories, going back decades, it is not always *world-famous artists such as the painters Pichler and Attersee, or the Nobel Prize winner Elias Canetti, who are to be found sitting there. On some evenings it is only creatively dressed coffee-house tourists who lurk there, regarding one other admiringly, as artists.*

III.

Kehren wir dennoch zurück zu Max Frisch. Er hätte mit Harry Webers Lichtbildern Freude gehabt. Denn diese sind alles andere als Adabei-Bilder. Sie ermutigen kein Schau-Gelüst dieser Art. Der ganze Bildband ist eine „visuelle Preisung des Schönen" (Ernst Haas), und das Schöne ist die Stadt Wien bei Nacht, ihre anonymen Witzbolde und Trauerweiden und, im Kapitel „Nacht-Arbeit", ihre ärmsten Paraberer.

Diese Photographien sind nicht Geschwätz über Menschen. Sie sind „Vision". Zunächst die Vision des Herrn Weber. Zugleich aber eine Ahnung unseres eigenen höheren Bildes vom nächtlichen Wien. So könnten wir Wien auch sehen. Wir müßten nur lernen, unseren abendmüden Blick vom Pflaster zu heben.

Die Kunststücke von Harry Weber brauchten das richtige Licht und die richtige Stunde, dazu oft ein richtiges Glück. Sie sind daher notwendig von einem Mann geschaffen, der gut mit sich selbst zurande kommt und einsam sein kann.

Die Summe des geduldigen Werks ist das größte Kompliment, das die Wienerstadt erfahren kann: daß sie selbst in den finstern Stunden prächtig ist. Tausende Details kommen gerade in der Nacht aus den Schatten ans Licht.

IV.

Die Texte dieses Buches sind nur ein roter Spagat, eingeflochten in den schimmernden Zopf der Weber-Bilder. Es gelten hier nicht die gleichen Gesetze der Eleganz.

Beispielsweise stellen wir gern die Frage: Macht die Wiener Nacht blöd? Erhebt oder erniedrigt uns ein Spaziergang von 7 bis 7, der beispielsweise von einem frühen Dinner beim witzigsten Italiener, Celestino Conte in der Kurrentgasse, bis zu einem sehr späten Frühstück beim „Drechsler" am Naschmarkt führt?

Es wäre kurzweiliger, könnten wir eine kurze, harte Antwort geben. Tatsächlich aber bleibt uns eine gewisse Balance nicht erspart. Teils-teils also. Gescheites und Umnachtetes halten sich die Waage.

Zunächst einmal: Wien hat seinen fairen Anteil an Dumpfgummis, da fährt die Eisenbahn drüber. Man kann Pech haben und zuviele auf einmal treffen. Dann hat man die Ohren voll barem Schund. Dann schreit man vor Schmerz, heult Rotz und Wasser und ist am nächsten Morgen nervlich fertig. Dann hat man seine Endzeitstimmung weg. Dann hält man Wien für den Arsch der Welt.

Doch Vorsicht ist geboten. Viele, die New York angeblich so gut kennen, rühmen die höhere Brillanz des Geisteslebens. Wer aber sein Englisch genug polierte, um alles halbwegs zu verstehen, kommt zu dem gleichen Schluß wie in Wien: Ein göttliches Gesetz will es, daß es zu jedem Liebenden einen Zerstörenden, zu jedem Herzensgebildeten einen Witzeerzähler, zu jedem Denkenden einen Illustriertenleser, zu jedem Interessierten einen Verdränger, zu jedem Hörenden einen Schwätzer, zu jedem Genie einen menschlichen Hydranten gibt.

III.

But let us return to Max Frisch. He would have enjoyed Harry Weber's photographs. For these are anything but limelight photographs. They do not encourage rubbernecks. The whole volume is a "visual eulogy of the Beautiful" (Ernst Haas), and the Beautiful is the city of Vienna by night, its anonymous jokers and sourpusses, and, in the chapter `Night Work', also its poorest grafters.

These photographs are not gossip about people. They are vision. First and foremost, the vision of Mr. Weber. At the same time, however, they are an intimation of our own higher image of nocturnal Vienna. We too can see Vienna in this way. We only have to learn to raise our eyes from the pavement.

Harry Weber's feats require the right light and the right hour, as well as a good deal of luck. They are thus necessarily the work of a man who is able to be alone and handle things on his own.

The sum total of this patient work is the greatest compliment that the city of Vienna could receive: that it is magnificent in the dark hours. Thousands of details emerge from the shadows, particularly at night.

IV.

The text of this book is only a red thread plaited into the shimmering braid of Weber's photographs. The same laws of elegance do not apply to both.

For instance, we like to ask the question: does the Viennese night make one stupid? Does a walk from 7 to 7 elevate or debase us, when it begins with, for example, early dinner at the amusing Italian restaurant Celestino Conte in the Kurrentgasse, and ends with a late breakfast at Drechsler in the Naschmarkt?

It would be more entertaining if we could provide a short, sharp answer. In actual fact, however, we cannot avoid a certain equilibrium. It is partly this, partly that. What is sensible and what is deranged tend to balance each other out.

First of all: Vienna has its fair share of morons, that is certain. But one can also be unlucky and meet too many at once. Then one has an ear full of pure trash. Then one screams with pain, cries bucketfuls and is a nervous wreck the next day. Then one's apocalyptic mood is over. Then one regards Vienna as the back of beyond.

Yet caution is advisable. Many people who are supposed to be well-acquainted with New York extol the greater brilliance of its intellectual life. Yet anyone who polishes up his English enough to understand most of what is being said, comes to the same conclusion as he would in Vienna: a divine law decrees that there is a destructive person for every lover, a teller of jokes for every person well-versed in matters of the heart, a reader of the illustrated magazines for every thinker, a person with a suppression complex for every interested person, a chatterbox for every listener, a human hydrant for every genius.

There are perhaps two main differences between Vienna and New York. The peaks can be higher and the valleys deeper there

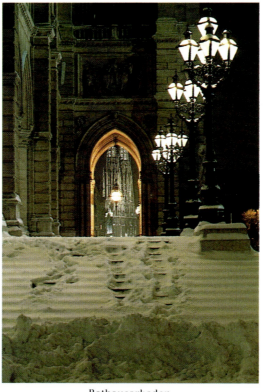

Rathausarkaden.
City Hall arcades

Vielleicht gibt es zwei Unterschiede zu New York. Die Spitzen könnten dort höher, die Täler tiefer sein als in Wien, weil es fünfmal so viele Menschen gibt. Und vielleicht fällt alles Blöde in Wien so auf, weil es in extrem schöner, geschichtlich tiefer Umgebung einen grauenvollen Kontrast liefert.

Gestern beobachteten wir mit unparteiischem Ekel eine fesche Schickimicki-Kuh mit ihrem neureichen Ochsen. Er erzählte, wie sensationell billig die tschechisch-slowakischen Hilfskräfte seien. Sie antwortete auf jeden seiner Sätze mit einem schrillen „Spitze!". Beide standen vor der säuberungsbedürftigen, aber noblen Kirche „Maria am Gestade". Dieses Gotteshaus hat eine stolze Gestalt und ist zirka ein halbes Jahrtausend älter als Amerika.

Wenn dieses Paar vor dem schwarzen Trump-Tower an der Fifth Avenue stünde, wäre es schlimm genug. Vor Maria am Gestade aber ist es das Letzte.

Vielleicht liegt es an dieser unerträglichen Diskrepanz von alt-edler Umwelt und oft enttäuschenden Passanten, daß sich viele Wien-bei-Nacht-Wanderer vereinzelten. Sie zogen mit Schreibblock, Zeichenblock, Kamera oder einfach einem guten Taschenbuch ihre einsame Spur. Das sind die nachtarbeitenden Denkerdarsteller von Wien.

„Die brauchen zum Alleinsein Gesellschaft", spottete Alfred Polgar.

V.

Es ist indes nicht immer klug, sich abzuschotten. Denn ab und zu gibt es Momente größter Ergriffenheit, die ungeplant aufstehen und unvergeßlich bleiben. An jenem Abend, als der deutsche Journalist zugegen war, spielte der nunmehr verstorbene Qualtinger aus dem Stegreif eine Nazi-Verhandlung, zugleich die Rolle des Angeklagten, des Klägers, des Richters.

Der deutsche Gast verabschiedete sich undeutlich. Es klang wie schönste Nacht des Lebens.

Der Bildband gibt eine Vorstellung, daß dafür nicht unbedingt Prominente notwendig sind, die den Weg kreuzen. Für jene, die gelernt haben, mit den Augen zu hören, spricht die große Stadt für sich selbst.

than they can in Vienna, because there are five times as many people. And perhaps one only tends to notice everything which is stupid in Vienna because it presents such a ghastly contrast to the city's extremely beautiful surroundings and depth of history.

Yesterday we observed with impartial disgust a smart trendy cow with her nouveau riche *ox. He told of how sensationally cheap Czechoslovakian labour was. She answered every sentence he spoke with a shrill: "Super!". Both of them were standing in front of the church of Maria am Gestade, which is elegant, even if it is in need of restoration. This house of God has a proud form and is roughly half a millenium older than America.*

If this couple had been standing in front of the black Trump Tower on Fifth Avenue, it would have been bad enough. But in front of Maria am Gestade – what could be worse!

Perhaps it is due to this insufferable discrepancy between an old and noble environment and passers-by who are often disappointing that many of the Vienna-by-night wanderers become loners. They go their own lonely ways with notepads, sketchpads, cameras or simply with a good paperback book. They are Vienna's thinker-actors who work at night.

"They need company to be alone", scorned Alfred Polgar.

V.

Yet it is not always very clever to isolate oneself. For, now and again, there are moments of the greatest emotion, which arise unplanned and remain unforgettable. On that evening with the German journalist, the now-deceased Qualtinger extemporised a Nazi trial, himself playing all the roles of defendant, prosecution and judge.

The German visitor bade an unintelligible farewell. It sounded as if it had been the most beautiful night of his life.

The present volume of photographs conveys the idea that it is not absolutely necessary to have prominent people cross one's path. For those who have learnt to listen with their eyes, the big city speaks for itself.

PANORAMEN
Vorhergehende Doppelseite: Blick vom Hochhaus in der Herrengasse auf die Innenstadt mit Peterskirche, Jesuitenkirche und Stephansdom
Links: Stadtpanorama vom Leopoldsberg mit den beleuchteten Türmen des Stephansdoms und der Kirche Maria am Gestade sowie den Kuppeln der Karlskirche und der Hofburg
Folgende Doppelseite: Blick vom Leopoldsberg auf die Donau und die nördlichen Stadtbezirke (XXI. und XXII.) mit dem Donauturm
Seite 16 (von links oben nach rechts unten): Kahlenberg und Leopoldsberg; Blick von der Flughafenautobahn auf die Raffinerie Schwechat; Blick vom Leopoldsberg auf den II. Bezirk und den Prater mit beleuchtetem Riesenrad; Blick von der Währinger Straße auf Schottenpassage, Schottenring und Neue Universität; Blick vom Laaerberg über den Richtfunkturm im Arsenal auf die UNO-City; Blick vom Hochhaus am Matzleinsdorfer Platz auf die Triester Straße

PANORAMIC VIEWS
Preceding double page: View across the inner city from Herrengasse, showing the Peterskirche, the Jesuitenkirche and St. Stephen's Cathedral
Left: Panorama of the city from Leopoldsberg, with the floodlit spire of St. Stephen's, the church of Maria am Gestade (St. Mary on the Riverbank) and the cupolas of the Karlskirche and the Hofburg
Following double page: View from Leopoldsberg, showing the Danube, the northern Districts (XXI and XXII) and the Danube Tower
Page 16 (from top left to bottom right): Kahlenberg and Leopoldsberg; Schwechat oil refinery, seen from the motorway to Schwechat Airport; View from Leopoldsberg of the II. District and the Prater, with the floodlit Ferris wheel; The Schottenpassage, Schottenring and the New University, seen from Währingerstraße; View from Laaerberg of the directional transmitter tower in the Arsenal and the UNO-City; View of the Triester Straße from Matzleinsdorfer Platz.

Wie ehrlich darf man zur eigenen Lieblingsstadt sein? Tatsache ist: Die Nachtschönheit Wiens erschließt sich in der Vogelschau nicht ohne weiteres. Der Blick über das Ostufer deprimiert durch die geradlinige Spärlichkeit der Lichter. Besser schon, wenn die Donau selbst mit im Bild ist. Dann bieten die Lichtschnüre der durchs Teleobjektiv eng gestaffelten Brücken die Verheißung von Leben. Einzigartig freilich der Blick vom Kahlenberg. Dann heben, wie der Kilimandjaro aus den Ebenen Afrikas, die Sehenswürdigkeiten wie gut verteilte Kerzen ihr Haupt – Stephansdom, Maria am Gestade, Karlskirche und Hofburg. Nacht-Wien wird mit jedem Meter, den man näherkommt, schöner.

How honest is one allowed to be about one's own favourite city? The fact is, that Vienna's nocturnal beauties do not reveal themselves in a bird's-eye-view straight away. The view across the east bank is depressing, on account of the straight line of sparse lights. It is better when the Danube itself is also in the picture. Then the string of lights on the bridges, closely stacked by the telescopic lens, offers a promise of life. However, the view from Kahlenberg is unique. Then – like Kilimanjaro from the plains of Africa – the sights raise their heads like well-arranged candles: St. Stephen's Cathedral, Maria am Gestade, the Karlskirche and the Hofburg. Night-time Vienna becomes more beautiful with every metre one covers in approaching it.

Nacht-Schönheit *Night Beauties*

Die Schönheit der Wiener Nacht ist zu empfinden wie eine Novelle, in der das Weite und Enge, das Gerade und Gewundene, das Sachliche und Kitschige in größter Musikalität nebeneinander wohnen.

Innere Erhebungen werden möglich. Warum kann es so berückend sein, beispielsweise mit dem schmalen Handke-Bändchen „Versuch über den geglückten Tag" durch eine geglückte Wiener Nacht zu gehen? Das sollte idealerweise in der Vorsaison oder der Nachsaison sein, mit nicht zu vielen Touristen auf den Straßen, auch nicht zu vielen Wienern. Der Schritt müßte ausgreifen können. Der flinke Fuß wäre angesagt, ein möglichst stundenlanger Eilmarsch um den Ring herum, dieses umwerfende Ensemble von Gründerzeit und herzigen Zahnlücken und ganz wenigen, unbedingt notwendigen Scheußlichkeiten. Dann müßte der Wanderer, wenn schon müde, kühn vorstoßen in den Kern der City, alle Schlupfwege nützend, die engen Passagen und witzigen Abschneider.

Die Winkelromantik, die wir so reich in den Außenbezirken finden, in Heurigenvierteln wie in Arbeitervierteln, findet der Kenner auch in der City. Sehr einnehmend beispielsweise die Schönlaterngasse. Sie hat keinen einzigen geraden Meter, nur Linkskurven und Rechtskurven, mit entzückenden Wirtshäusern und Antiquariaten. Der große Mime Helmut Qualtinger war dort zuhause.

Das Gewurl wohnt nahe den großen Lichtplätzen. Oft geht der Wanderer aus dem Halbdunkel eines Laternenplätzchens um die nächste Ecke und prallt zurück, als hätte jemand wie im Filmatelier Scheinwerfer und Ton angeschaltet. Dann öffnen sich der Hohe Markt, der Neue Markt, der Kohlmarkt, der Graben – oder die Kärnterstraße. Sie ist die immer noch elegante Schlagader Wiens. Jetzt schon lange Fußgängerzone, ist sie Geldquelle internationaler Straßenmusikanten. Manchmal mischen sich bedürftige Österreicher dazu. Einer davon, ein Saxophonist, verfolgte den Beobachter mit einem jedem Ausländer unverständlichen „Küß-die-Hand", von Mann zu Mann, weil nicht eine Münze, sondern eine Banknote in der Geldkappe gelandet war.

Die Schönheit der Wiener Nacht hat freilich mehr Gesichter als der legendäre Sir Laurence Olivier: Eine grüne Schubertsche Lindenbaumromantik in den Nobelbezirken; ein polyglotter Glanz des umstrittenen Stephansplatzes, wo der würdige Dom und das postmoderne Haas-Haus konkurrieren; eine für manche reizvolle Kargheit der sogenannten Arbeiterbezirke; und eine spezielle herbe Stadtschönheit, die sich sonst nur mehr den Liebhabern des ehemaligen Ost-Berlin erschließt: die derzeit noch recht zerrissene Gegend über der Donau, Transdanubien genannt.

Der Stephansdom, das Wahrzeichen Wiens.
St. Stephen's, Vienna's most prominent landmark

The beauty of the Viennese night should be experienced like a novella in which the expansive and the restricted, the straight and the crooked, the factual and the trashy coexist with the greatest musicality.

Inner elation is possible. What makes it so fascinating to walk through a successful Viennese night with, for example, the slim Handke volume Versuch über den geglückten Tag *('Essay on the Successful Day')? Ideally, it should be in the pre-season or the off-season, with not too many tourists on the streets, nor too many Viennese. One must be able to take long strides. Light feet would be recommended, a forced march (lasting several hours if possible) around the Ring, that fantastic ensemble dating from the Gründerzeit, with sweet little gaps between its teeth and a very few – absolutely necessary – monstrosities. Then the wanderer, even if he or she is already tired, must bravely push on into the inner city, taking advantage of all the back-ways, narrow passages and funny short-cuts.*

The romantic winding streets, so many of which we find in the suburbs (both in the Heurigen *Districts and the working-class Districts), can also be found in the inner city, if one knows where to look. Very attractive, for example, is the Schönlaterngasse. It does not contain a single straight metre, only left and right turns, with delightful pubs and restaurants and second-hand bookshops. This is where the great mime Helmut Qualtinger used to live.*

The teeming throng dwells near to the large and well-lit squares. Emerging from the half-dark of a small, lantern-lit square, the wanderer often walks round the next corner only to recoil as if someone had suddenly turned on the floodlights and sound in a film studio. Then there opens out before him the Hohe Markt, the Neue Markt, the Kohlmarkt, the Graben – or the Kärntnerstraße. The last is still the most elegant artery in Vienna. It has long since become a pedestrian area and is now a source of income for street musicians of all nationalities. Sometimes there are also needy Austrians among them. One of them, a saxophonist, shouted after a spectator, man to man: "Küß-die-Hand" (incomprehensible to every foreigner) simply because it was not a coin but a banknote which had landed in his money cap.

Of course, the beauty of the Viennese night has more faces than Sir Laurence Olivier: green Schubertian linden-tree romanticism in the posh Districts; the polyglot splendour of the controversial Stephansplatz, where the dignified cathedral and the post-modern Haas-Haus compete together; the barrenness – attractive to some – of the so-called working-class Districts; and an especially austere city sight, whose beauty is now only appreciated by lovers of East Berlin: the area, at present quite dilapidated, on the other side of the Danube, known as 'Transdanubia'.

DER STEPHANSDOM
Links (von links oben nach rechts unten): Stephansturm vom Graben; Maria Pötsch-Altar im rechten Seitenschiff; Blick zum Hochaltar; Stephansturm vom Petersplatz

Rechts: Blick auf die Türme von Michaelerkirche und Stephansdom sowie die Michaelerkuppel der Hofburg

*ST. STEPHEN'S CATHEDRAL
Left (from top left to bottom right):
St. Stephen's Cathedral seen from the Graben; Altar in the right aisle, dedicated to Our Lady of Pócz; High altar; St. Stephen's from Petersplatz*

Right: The spires of the Michaelkirche and St. Stephen's and the cupola of the Hofburg

DER STOCK IM EISEN-PLATZ
Links: Der Stephansplatz vom Haas-Haus in Richtung Rotenturmstraße

Rechts: Das neue Haas-Haus am Stephansplatz

STOCK-IM-EISEN-PLATZ
Left: Stefansplatz and Rotenturmstraße, seen from the Haas-Haus

Right: The new Haas-Haus in Stefansplatz

DIE KÄRNTNER STRASSE
Links: Blick vom Opernring in Richtung Stephansplatz

Rechts: Blick vom Haas-Haus in die weihnachtlich geschmückte Kärntner Straße

KÄRNTNER STRASSE
Left: View of Stefansplatz from the Opernring

Right: View from the Haas-Haus of the Kärntner Straße, decorated for Christmas

Das zentrale magnetische Hufeisen der Stadt sind Kärntner Straße und Kohlmarkt, im Nordosten verbunden durch den Graben. Die Kärntner Straße ist das längste Stück: früher die Flaniermeile reicher Söhne, die ihre MGAs und 190 SL und Porsche 356 spazierenführten, heute ein hochfrequentierter Fußgängerparcours mit eleganten teuren Geschäften und billiger Straßenmusik. Der nächtliche Flaneur könnte nach dem Opernbesuch summend in den Südzipfel der „Kärntner" eindringen. Ein paar hundert Auslagen später, am anderen Zipfel, erwartet der Stephansdom ein frommes Gesicht. Dann lockt der querliegende Graben, oder die Rotenturmstraße, die hinunterführt zum Bermudadreieck.

The Kärntnerstraße and Kohlmarkt, connected in the north-east by the Graben, form the city's central magnetic horseshoe. The Kärntnerstraße is the longest part: formerly the mile where wealthy sons would drive along flaunting their MGAs, 190 SLs and Porsche 356s, it is today a very well-frequented obstacle course for pedestrians, with elegant and expensive shops and cheap street music. Humming after a visit to the Opera, the nocturnal stroller might enter 'the Kärntner' at its southern end. A couple of hundred shop-windows later, at the other end, is St. Stephen's Cathedral, expecting a pious face. There, one is tempted by the Graben, which runs across it, or the Rotenturmstraße, which leads down to the Bermuda Triangle.

DER GRABEN
Blick vom Kohlmarkt über die Pestsäule in Richtung Stock-im-Eisen-Platz

GRABEN
View from Kohlmarkt of the Plague Column and Stock-im-Eisen-Platz

Der Graben ist an Sommerabenden laut, dennoch ein Hauptplatz des Geistes. Wie schön, daß auf dem teuersten Fleck so viele gute Buchhandlungen existieren. Thomas Bernhard saß da gern auf einem Bankerl. Er muß einen seltsamen Frieden empfunden haben, wie im Auge des Zyklons.

The Graben is noisy on summer evenings, even though it is of great importance intellectually. How nice to have so many good bookshops on such an expensive spot! Thomas Bernhard used to like to sit on one of the benches here. He must have experienced a strange peace, as if watching from the eye of the cyclone.

STRASSENLEBEN
Rechts (von links oben
nach rechts unten):
Window-shopping im
Flanierbereich der
Innenstadt (Lugeck,
Graben, Stallburg-
gasse, Himmelpfort-
gasse)

Folgende Doppelseite:
Jeunesse und Sandler,
Straßenmusiker und
Luftballonverkäufer im
Bereich Kärntner
Straße, Stock-im-
Eisen-Platz und
Graben

STREET SCENES
Right (from top left to
bottom right): Window
shopping in the
pedestrian area of the
inner city (Lugeck,
Graben, Stallburg-
gasse, Himmelpfort-
gasse)

Following double page:
Youngsters and down-
and -outs, street
musicians and balloon
sellers in the shopping
area around Kärntner
Straße, Stock-im-Eisen-
Platz and Graben

GASSEN DER ALTSTADT
Links: Schönlaterngasse

Rechts (von links oben nach rechts unten): Haarhof; Blumenstockgasse; Kurrentgasse; Schulhof

STREETS OF THE OLD CITY
Left: Schönlaterngasse

Right (from top left to bottom right): Haarhof; Blumenstockgasse; Kurrentgasse; Schulhof

Alteuropäische Metropolen wie Wien, die auf sich halten, bieten dem Gast die Geborgenheit enger Gassen und enger Kurven. So kann man sie erstens leichter von Los Angeles unterscheiden. Zweitens bleibt die Geschwindigkeit des Nachtwanderers niedrig. Er beschleunigt und bremst, beschleunigt und bremst. In der Bremszone steht immer ein Wirtshaus und bietet höflich sein Service an. Die Verkehrssicherheit der Spaziergänger ist hoch, die Kriminalitätsrate niedrig, in den Außenbezirken wie in der Innenstadt. Auch das unterscheidet von Los Angeles.

The older self-respecting European capitals like Vienna provide visitors with the security of narrow streets and tight bends. First of all, this makes it easier to distinguish such cities from Los Angeles. Secondly, it keeps the night-bird's speed down. He accelerates and then brakes, accelerates and then brakes. In the braking zone there is always a pub which can obligingly offer its services. In both the suburbs and the inner city there is a high degree of road safety for the pedestrian, and the crime rate is low. And that is another difference to Los Angeles.

WIENER LATERNEN
Links (von links oben nach rechts unten): Heiligenkreuzer Hof; Maria-Theresien-Platz; Augustinerbastei; Rathausarkaden

Rechts: Radetzkybrücke bei der Urania

*VIENNESE STREET LAMPS
Left (from top left to bottom right): Heiligenkreuzer Hof; Maria-Theresien-Platz; Augustinerbastei ; City Hall arcade*

Right: The Radetzkybrücke, next to the Urania

CHRISTKINDLMÄRKTE
Links: Rathausturm mit Eisernem Rathausmann

Rechts: Weihnachtsmarkt in der Spittelberggasse (VII.)

CHRISTMAS FAIRS
Left: Spire of City Hall with the 'Iron Man'

Right: Christmas fair at Spittelberg (VII District)

Wer Wien bei Nacht erleben will, ist längst nicht mehr auf die zwei traditionellen Pole angewiesen – Innenstadt und Grinzing. Vor allem auch in der Kreisfläche zwischen Gürtel und Ring ist das Nachtleben dichter, alternativer und origineller geworden. Der Spittelberg beispielsweise gilt als interessanter Versuch, alte Bausubstanz und junge philosophische Geister zusammenzubringen. Ob aus der Idee ein Sieg oder eine Niederlage wurde, kann noch nicht wirklich beurteilt werden. Applaus ist gleichwohl angebracht. Wien hat sich endlich Experimenten aller Art geöffnet.

People wanting to experience Vienna by night are today no longer restricted solely to its two traditional poles: the city centre and Grinzing. Particularly in that part of the circle between the Gürtel and the Ring, night-life has become busier, more alternative and more original. Spittelberg, for example, is an interesting attempt to bring young and philosophical spirits to the old architectural substance. It is still too early to judge whether this idea will result in a victory or a defeat. Yet it deserves applause in any case. Vienna has at last opened itself up to experiments of all kinds.

TORE UND PASSAGEN
Oben (von links oben nach rechts unten): Singerstraße; Sonnenfelsgasse; Himmelpfortgasse (Winterpalais Prinz Eugen); Klimschgasse (III.); Mölkerbastei; Passage Wollzeile – Stephansplatz

Rechts: Passage Mariahilfer Straße – Windmühlgasse

GATES AND PASSAGES
Top (from top left to bottom right): Singerstraße; Sonnenfelsgasse; Himmelpfortgasse (Prince Eugene's Winter Palace); Klimschgasse (III District); Mölkerbastei; Passage Wollzeile – Stefansplatz

Right: Passage Mariahilfer Straße – Windmühlgasse

Viele Klischees rühren aus der Zeit, in der Wien die Hauptstadt eines Riesenreiches war, in dem die Sonne nie unterging. Spätestens ab der Zeit von Johann Strauß Vater und Johann Strauß Sohn und Josef Lanner gelten die Wiener als Geiger und Tänzer, und dank der „Fledermaus" als haltlose Schlucker und Nachtfalter. So entstand auch das bittere Vorurteil, die schmiedeeisernen Tore der Wiener Häuser seien kunstvoll und individuell, damit jeder beim Nachhausekommen seine Adresse erkenne. Das ist falsch. Kunstwerke sind's, weil jeder Wiener Kunstschmied ein Geiger und Tänzer ist.

There are many clichés deriving from the days when Vienna was the capital of a huge empire on which the sun never set. At the very latest by the time of Johann Strauß the Elder, Johann Strauß the Younger and Josef Lanner, the Viennese were considered to be fiddlers and dancers, and – thanks to the Fledermaus – also as incorrigible wine-bibbers and night-revellers. This gave rise to the bitter prejudice that the reason why the wrought-iron gates of Viennese houses were all so artistically and individually designed was to help people find their own addresses on their way home. This is untrue. They are such works of art because every Viennese metalwork craftsman is also a fiddler and a dancer.

GITTER
Links: Wohnstraße am Margaretenplatz (V.)

Rechts: Eingang unter dem Hochturm an der Südseite des Stephansdoms

GRILLS
Left: Residential street, Margaretenplatz (V District)

Right: South entrance to St. Stephen's Cathedral, situated below the great spire

KLEINE NACHTMUSIK
Links: Seiteneingang der
Staatsoper

Rechts: Staatsoper von der
Philharmonikergasse

LITTLE NIGHT MUSIC
Left: State Opera: Side entrance

*Right: State Opera from
Philharmonikergasse*

Ein Lieblingsbild des Texters
und des Verlegers. Leider auch
Beweis für den unmenschlichen
Fleiß und düsteren Charakter
des Photographen. Der Geiger
wurde nachgestellt! Damit diese
subtile Abstufung von tief-
violettem Nachthimmel vor
schwarzem Haus möglich
wurde, mußte der Violinist
gebeten werden, endlich
stillzustehen.

*One of the favourite photographs
of both the author and the
publisher. Unfortunately, it is
also evidence of the inhuman
industriousness and character of
the photographer. The fiddler
has adopted a pose! In order to
obtain the subtle gradation of the
dark-violet night sky in front of
the black house, the violinist
finally had to be asked to stand
still for a while.*

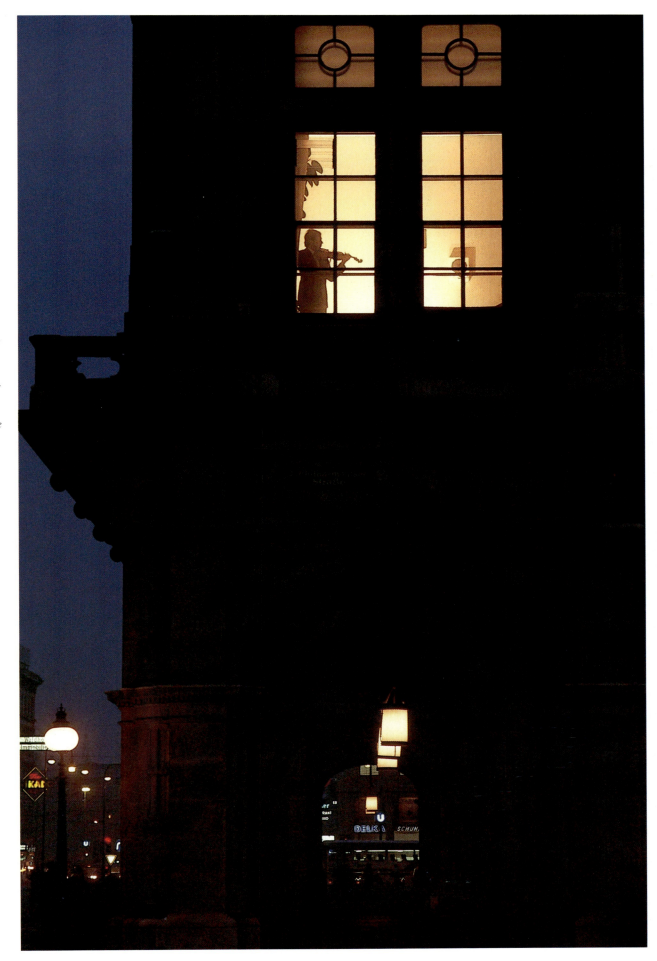

BELEUCHTETE FENSTER
Links: Vollmond in der Vorstadt (XV.)

Rechts: Churhaus am Stephansplatz

ILLUMINATED WINDOWS
Left: Full moon in Vienna (XV District)

Right: The Churhaus, in Stefansplatz

DIE HOFBURG
Links: Blick vom Kohlmarkt auf die Michaelerkirche und die Michaelerkuppel des Inneren Burgtors

Rechts: Bekrönungen des Reichskanzleitrakts am Platz In der Burg (oben und unten); Doppeladler am Mittelrisalit der Neuen Burg (Mitte)

THE HOFBURG
Left: View of the Michaelerkirche and the cupola of the inner gate to the Hofburg, seen from Kohlmarkt

Right: Façade decoration of the Reichskanzleitrakt of the Hofburg in the Platz In der Burg (above and below); Double eagle on the central projection of the Neue Burg (centre)

SCHWEIZERHOF UND STALLBURG
Oben (von links nach rechts): Schweizertor in der Hofburg; Schweizerhof; Monumentalbrunnen „Macht zur See" am Michaelertrakt der Hofburg

Rechts: Lipizzaner auf dem Weg von der Stallburg in die Winterreitschule

SCHWEIZERHOF AND STALLBURG
Above (from left to right): Schweizertor (Swiss Gate) in the Hofburg; Schweizerhof (Swiss Yard); Monumental fountain Power at Sea in front of the Michaelertrakt of the Hofburg

Right: The famous Lipizzaner horses on their way from Stallburg (Imperial Stables) to the Winter Riding School

Hofburgkapelle und Michaelerplatz (herrliche Melange im wiedererweckten Café Griensteidl!) sind uns lieb und wert, aber blicken wir nach rechts. Wir befinden uns in der Stallburg. Eintritt nur für weiße Pferde in Begleitung ihrer Diener.

Although the Hofburgkapelle and Michaelerplatz are both very dear to us, we nevertheless glance to the right. We are here in the Stallburg. Entrance reserved for white horses accompanied by their servants.

Heldenplätze sind nicht mehr beschreibbar. Die eindrucksvolle Schale kann nicht vom Kern gelöst werden, der immer atavistisch, friedensfern und schwül ist. Im Falle des Heldenplatzes von Wien werden ästhetische Empfindungen unter das schwere Wasser der Geschichte gedrückt, der älteren wie der jüngeren.
Wie schön, gäbe es einen vergleichbaren „Platz der Nobelpreisträger Österreichs", zeigend die gleiche Großzügigkeit eines Bauherrn, das Genie der Architekten und die köstliche, handwerklich so unendlich schwierige Balance der Denkmäler. Wir stellen uns aber gerne einen Wanderer aus fernen Ländern vor, der unbelastet von Österreichs Geschichte, Politik und Kultur die Wiener Nacht bereist. Er kommt aus der eng gebauten Altstadt durchs Michaelertor auf eine weite, begrünte Fläche, nimmt die Stille des Platzes zur Beruhigung der Seele auf und zählt die Sterne des Himmels, der hier größer ist als an jedem anderen Punkt der Inneren Stadt.

Squares dedicated to a country's heroes defy description today. The impressive shell cannot be separated from the kernel, which is atavistic, oppressive and far from peace-loving. In the case of Vienna's Heldenplatz, aesthetic sensations are weighed down by the heavy water of history, that of both the distant and the more recent past.
How nice it would be if there were a comparable 'Square of Austrian Nobel Prize Winners', displaying the same generosity of patronage and architectural genius, with that same superb balance of the monuments, which it is so infinitely difficult for the craftsman to achieve.
However, we also like to imagine a traveller from a distant country who wanders through the Viennese night without being burdened by the history, politics and culture of Austria. Emerging from the narrow streets of the old town through the Michaelertor, he comes out into an expansive, grassy area, absorbs the quietness of the square as a way of soothing his soul, and counts the stars in the sky, more of which are visible from here than at any other point in the city.

AM HELDENPLATZ
Prinz-Eugen-Denkmal vor der Neuen Burg auf dem Heldenplatz

HELDENPLATZ
Equestrian statue of Prince Eugene in front of the Neue Burg in Heldenplatz

DENKMÄLER
Links: Schiller-Denkmal vor der Akademie der bildenden Künste auf dem Schillerplatz

Rechts: Mozart-Denkmal im Burggarten

STATUES
Left: Statue of Friedrich von Schiller in front of the Akademie der bildenden Künste (Academy of Fine Arts)

Right: Mozart monument in the Burggarten

FASSADEN
Links: Die Staatsoper vom Opernring, im Hintergrund das Hotel Bristol

Rechts (von links oben nach rechts unten): Blick von der Neustiftgasse auf das Naturhistorische Museum, im Vordergrund das Volkstheater (VII.); Doppeladler-Skulptur auf der Kennedy-Brücke (XIII.); Blick vom Haarhof auf das Länderbank-Gebäude am Hof; Firstfiguren auf dem Kohlmarkt

FAÇADES
Left: The State Opera, seen from the Opernring, with Hotel Bristol in the background

Right (from top left to bottom right): The Naturhistorisches Museum (Museum of Natural History), seen from Neustiftgasse, with the Volkstheater (VII District) in the foreground; Sculpture of the double eagle on the Kennedy-Brücke (XIII District); The Länderbank, seen from Haarhof; Figures on a roof in Kohlmarkt

DIE STAATSOPER
Die Staatsoper von der Albertina-Rampe, im Vordergrund das Erzherzog-Albrecht-Denkmal

STATE OPERA
The State Opera, seen from the ramp of the Albertina, with the equestrian statue of Archduke Albrecht in the foreground

Vorne, an der Balustrade, standen wir mit dem Publizisten Stephan Vajda. Er hatte mit „Felix Austria" gerade das lebhafteste Geschichtswerk Österreichs geschrieben. Sein Glück war grenzenlos, er umarmte die ganze Welt. Daß er so bald danach sterben würde, war undenkbar. Da stand er also auf der Albertina-Rampe und gab die endgültige Definition dieses Standorts: „Ich bin von Wundern umgeben. In meinem Rücken das Wunder der größten Graphiksammlung der Welt. Rechts von mir das Wunder der Wiener Oper, in der die wunderbarsten Sänger trotz des grausamsten Publikums der Welt auftreten. Und links vorne das Hotel Sacher, mit der blauen Bar und diesem wunderbaren Marc de Bourgogne."

We are seen here in the foreground, standing by the balustrade, with the publicist Stephan Vajda. He was the author of what is probably the most vivid history of Austria that has been written, namely Felix Austria. His happiness was infinite, he embraced the whole world. The fact that he would die soon afterwards was unthinkable. He thus stood there on the ramp of the Albertina and gave the ultimate definition of this location: "I am surrounded by wonders. Behind me is the wonder of the largest collection of graphic art in the world. To my right the wonder of the Vienna Opera, where the greatest singers perform, despite having to appear before the most dreadful audience in the world. And in front of me, to my left, is Hotel Sacher, with its blue bar and that wonderful Marc de Bourgogne."

DER OPERNBALL
Links: „Alles Walzer"

Rechts: Eröffnungswalzer des Jungdamen- und Jungherrenkomitees

THE OPERA BALL
Left: "Alles Walzer"

Right: Opening waltz of
the debutantes and
their partners

WIENER TANZ-
VERGNÜGEN
Links (von links oben
nach rechts unten):
Blick aus einer
Opernball-Loge;
Ballproben in der
Tanzschule Willy
Elmayer-Vestenbrugg;
Eröffnung des Opern-
balls

Rechts: Treppenhaus
der Staatsoper

*DANCING IN VIENNA
Left (from top left to bottom right): View from a box at the Opera Ball; Rehearsal for the opening of the Opera Ball in the renowned dancing school of Willy Elmayer-Vestenbrugg; Opening of the Opera Ball*

Right: Staircase at the Opera House

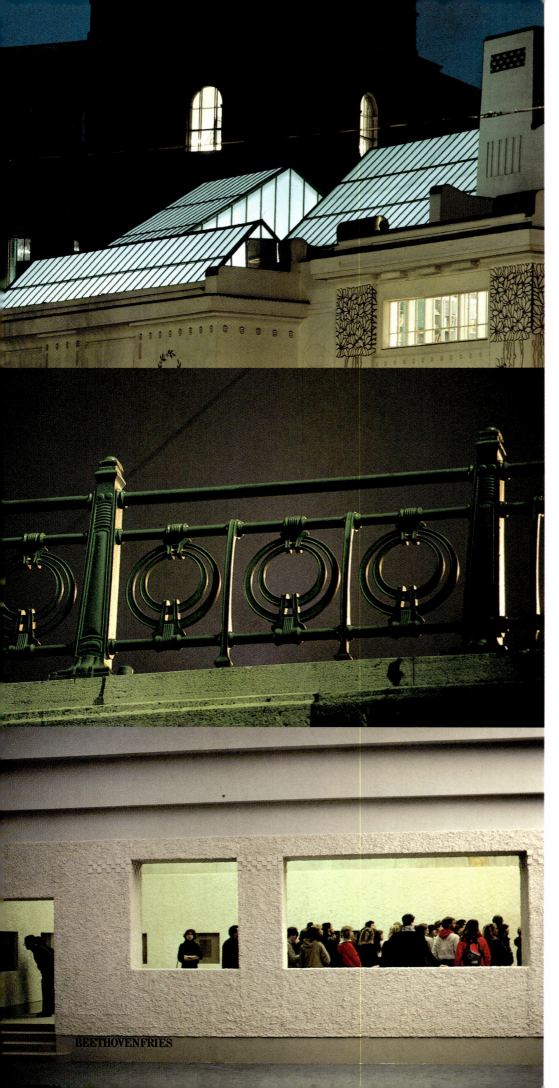

WIENER JUGENDSTIL
Links (von oben nach unten): Secession; Geländer der Radetzkybrücke; Gustav Klimts Beethoven-Fries im Souterrain der Secession

Rechts: Wienfluß-Portal im Stadtpark

*VIENNESE JUGENDSTIL
Left (top to bottom): Secession; Railings of the Radetzkybrücke; The Beethoven Frieze by Gustav Klimt (in the basement of the Secession)*

Right: Wienfluss Gates in the Stadtpark

Es gibt Wiener Intellektuelle – Sammelbegriff für alle, die beim Lesen nicht die Lippen bewegen -, die den Jugendstil ablehnen, weil er im Ausland zu Österreichs Ruf beiträgt.
Wir bewegen lieber die Lippen und sagen: schön, daß er da ist. Dies fällt umso leichter, als wir nächtelang dem Joseph „Seppi" Ziegler zuhörten, einem maßgeblichen Metallurgen und Restaurator. Sein leicht makabres Hauptamt ist zwar die perfekte Konservierung der Kapuzinergruft. Aber er ist auch an Jugendstil-Erhaltungsarbeiten beteiligt, deren Ernsthaftigkeit und Genauigkeit Freude macht.

*There are Viennese intellectuals – a collective term for all those who do not move their lips when reading – who reject Jugendstil because it contributes to Austria's image abroad.
We prefer to move our lips and say: it's good that it's there. This became that much easier after we spent several nights listening to Joseph 'Sepp' Ziegler, a leading metallurgist and restorer. His slightly macabre principal job is the perfect conservation of the Capuchin Crypt. But he is also involved in the preservation of Jugendstil works, and his seriousness and exactitude is a joy to see.*

RINGSTRASSEN-
DENKMÄLER
Rechts: Goethe-
Denkmal am Opern-
ring/Ecke Goethegasse
Folgende Doppelseite:
Erzherzog-Carl-
Denkmal auf dem
Heldenplatz, im
Hintergrund das
Äußere Burgtor und
die Kuppel des
Kunsthistorischen
Museums

MONUMENTS ON THE
RINGSTRASSE
Right: Statue of Johann
Wolfgang von Goethe,
on the Opernring/
corner of Goethegasse
Following double page:
Equestrian statue of
Archduke Karl in
Heldenplatz, with the
outer Burgtor and the
cupola of the Kunst-
historisches Museum
(Art History Museum)
in the background

Goethe belebt. Zu ihm fällt vielen was ein. Vier denkwürdige Nachtmomente mit Denkmalschauern:
1. Besucher des nahegelegenen Burgkinos: „Besser eine Lauren Bacall als drei Gretchen."
2. Ein Pensionst rezitiert elendslang und eitel, aber gar nicht schlecht aus Goethes Werken, unter anderem „Die Bürgschaft".
3. Abteilung guterzogene, gebildete, goscherte Teenager: „Wir haben der Welt klargemacht, daß Beethoven uns, dafür der Hitler den Deutschen gehört. Ist der Goethe auch schon ein Wiener?"
4. Gleiche Abteilung: „So wie er da liegt, hat er die ‚Wahlverwandtschaften' nie geschrieben."

Goethe inspires. One always thinks of something in connection with him. Four memorable night moments with spectators of his monument:
1. Visitors to the nearby Burg cinema: "Better a Lauren Bacall than three Gretchens."
2. A pensioner gives an interminably long and conceited, (although not actually bad) recital from Goethe's work, including Die Bürgschaft ('The Surety').
3. Department of well-brought up, educated, cheeky teenagers: "We have shown the world that Beethoven belongs to us and Hitler to the Germans. Wasn't Goethe Viennese too?"
4. Same department: "He could never have written the Elective Affinities lying there like that."

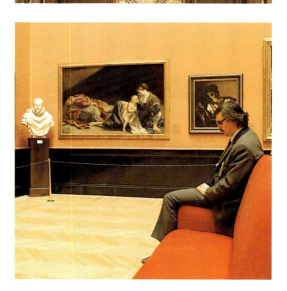

MUSEEN UND GALERIEN
Links (von oben nach unten): Galerie am Graben; Stiegenhaus des Kunsthistorischen Museums; Gemäldegalerie des Kunsthistorischen Museums

Rechts: Galerie Ulysses

MUSEUMS AND GALLERIES
Left (from top to bottom): Galerie am Graben; Staircase of the Kunsthistorisches Museum; Picture Gallery of the Kunsthistorisches Museum

Right: Galerie Ulysses

Wiens Galeriebesitzer haben dreierlei. Ein großes Verdienst um die Menschheit. Ein hartes Los wegen ihrer Berufsbezeichnung. Einen brutalen ersten Satz für Besucher.
Das Verdienst: Jede Vernissage jedweden Künstlers ist ein besserer Einstieg in die Nacht als alles andere (auch wenn es keine Vernissagen im klassischen Sinn sind: das Fixieren der Bilder vor Publikum).
Das harte Los: Ein Galerist ist in der Sprache der Polizei ein Gauner.
Der erste Satz: „Rotwein oder Weißwein?"

There are three things about Vienna's art gallery owners. They do a great service to mankind. They have a hard fate on account of their professional appellation. They have a brutal first sentence for visitors.
The service: every vernissage of any artist whatsoever is the best way of all to embark upon the night (even if there are no varnishing days in the classical sense of retouching the pictures in public).
The hard fate: in Viennese police slang, the word for 'gallery owner' (Galerist) is another name for a crook.
The first sentence: "Red wine or white wine?"

65

RINGSTRASSENBAUTEN
Links: Rampe des Justizpalasts auf dem Schmerlingplatz, im Hintergrund das Naturhistorische Museum

Rechts: Rampe des Parlaments mit Pallas-Athene-Brunnen, im Hintergrund die Dachfiguren des Burgtheaters

ARCHITECTURE ON THE
RINGSTRASSE
Left: Ramp of the Palace of
Justice in Schmerlingplatz, with
the Naturhistorisches Museum in
the background

Right: Ramp of Parliament and
the Pallas Athene Fountain, with
figures crowning the Burgtheater
façade in the background

DAS RATHAUS
Links: Standbild des Barockbaumeisters Johann Bernhard Fischer von Erlach auf dem Rathausplatz

Rechts: Turm des Rathauses von der Rampe des Parlaments

CITY HALL
Left: Statue of Baroque architect Johann Bernhard Fischer von Erlach in front of City Hall

Right: Spire of City Hall, seen from the ramp of Parliament

DACHLANDSCHAFTEN
Links: Dachfigur eines ungarischen Husaren am Graben/Ecke Kohlmarkt

Rechts: Allegorische Figur auf dem Dach des Burgtheaters

VIENNESE ROOFSCAPES
Left: Statue of a Hungarian Hussar on the roof of a house on the corner of Kohlmarkt and Graben

Right: Allegorical figure on the roof of the Burgtheater

Das Wunderbare und Makabre an der Wiener Architektur: Für wen sind die aufwendigen Details ganz oben geschaffen? Es könnte für die Götter sein, in der Art aller Naturalopfer. Wer die schönere Statue dem Himmel weiht, hat ein Ticket. Es könnte auch Noblesse der Hauseigentümer sein: Großer Aufwand selbst dort, wo man's nicht sieht. Der nächtliche Besucher Wiens weiß oft nicht, welche Mühe man sich mit der Gestaltung der Dächer gibt.

The wonderful and macabre thing about Viennese architecture: for whom are the intricate details right at the top actually intended? It might be for the gods, in the manner of all natural sacrifices. Someone who dedicates a beautiful statue to heaven, gets a ticket there. It might also be for the high-minded house owners: extravagance even where it cannot be seen. Nocturnal visitors to Vienna are often unaware of just how much trouble has been taken with the design of the roofs.

MUSIK- UND SPRECH-
THEATER
Vorhergehende
Doppelseite (von links
oben nach rechts
unten): Theater in der
Josefstadt; Kartenvor-
verkauf; Schönbrunner
Schloßtheater; Zu-
schauerraum der
Staatsoper (großes
Bild),

Links: Der Goldene
Saal des Musikvereins
mit den Wiener
Philharmonikern

Rechts (von links oben
nach rechts unten):
Stehparterre in der
Staatsoper; Garderobe
im Theater in der
Josefstadt; Bühnenein-
gang des Theaters in
der Josefstadt; Steh-
platzbesucher in den
Arkaden der Staatsoper

MUSIC AND THEATRE
Preceding double page
(from top left to bottom
right): Theater in der
Josefstadt; At the box-
office; Schönbrunn
Palace Theatre; State
Opera, auditorium
(large picture)

Left: Golden Hall of the
Wiener Musikverein,
with Vienna
Philharmonic
Orchestra

Right (from top left to
bottom right): Standing
room in the State
Opera; Theater in der
Josefstadt, dressing-
room; Theater in der
Josefstadt, stage
entrance; Queuing for
standing room tickets
under the arcades of
the State Opera

Marcel Prawy war eines übernächtigen Morgens der Sitznachbar beim Friseur, der in der Fuchsthallergasse vis-à-vis der Volksoper amtete. Prawy schien gut ausgeschlafen, war bester Laune. Die Rede kam auf seine zweite Leidenschaft neben dem Musiktheater, das Sammeln von Plastiksackerln.
Wenn wir ihn richtig verstanden haben, sind Plastiksackerln
a) schön, weil praktisch als Archiv
b) schön, weil praktisch als Klein-LKW
c) schön, weil ein Zeichen der Demut: wer das allabendliche Privileg habe, großen Menschen zuzuhören, brauche kein Eidechsenleder mehr.
Wir erzählen dies, weil Wien die westliche Metropole mit den meisten Plastiksackerlträgern ist, auch in der Nacht.

One hungover morning, Marcel Prawy was the person sitting next to me in the salon of that barber who officiates in the Fuchsthallergasse, opposite the Volksoper. Prawy seemed to have slept well and was in the best of moods. The conversation came round to his second love (after the theatre): that of collecting plastic bags.
If we understood him correctly, then plastic bags are
a) beautiful because they are practical as archives
b) beautiful because they are practical as vans
c) beautiful because they are a sign of humbleness: someone who has the privilege of listening to great people every evening no longer has any need of lizard leather.
We relate this because in Vienna more people carry plastic bags than in any other western metropolis – even at night.

AM RAND DER RINGSTRASSE
Links: Hochstrahlbrunnen auf dem Schwarzenbergplatz (III.)

Rechts: Die Mölkerbastei, im Hintergrund das Liebenberg-Denkmal und die Neue Universität

ALONG THE RING-STRASSE
Left: High-jet fountain at Schwarzenbergplatz (III District)

Right: Mölkerbastei (part of the former city ramparts), with the Liebenberg monument and the New University in the background

IM STIL DER RING-
STRASSE
Links: Die Votivkirche
(IX.), im Hintergrund
die Türme der
Piaristenkirche (VIII.)

Rechts (von oben nach
unten):
Dachbalustrade auf
dem Palais Todesco in
der Kärntner Straße;
Blick von der Weih-
burggasse auf das
Johann-Strauß-
Denkmal im Stadtpark;
Hotel Sacher

*THE RINGSTRASSE
STYLE
Left: Votivkirche (IX
District), with the
Piaristenkirche (VIII
District) in the
background*

*Right (from top to
bottom): Palais
Todesco, Kärntner
Straße: roof balustrade;
Statue of Johann
Strauß in Stadtpark;
Hotel Sacher*

DAS BELVEDERE
Blick vom Oberen Belvedere über den Belvedere-Park auf die Innenstadt

*BELVEDERE
View of Belvedere Gardens and the inner city, seen from Upper Belvedere*

WIENER BAROCK
Links: Oberes Belvedere (III.) von der Südseite

Rechts: Die Karlskirche (IV.)

*VIENNESE BAROQUE
Left: Upper Belvedere, seen from the south (III District)*

Right: The Karlskirche (IV District)

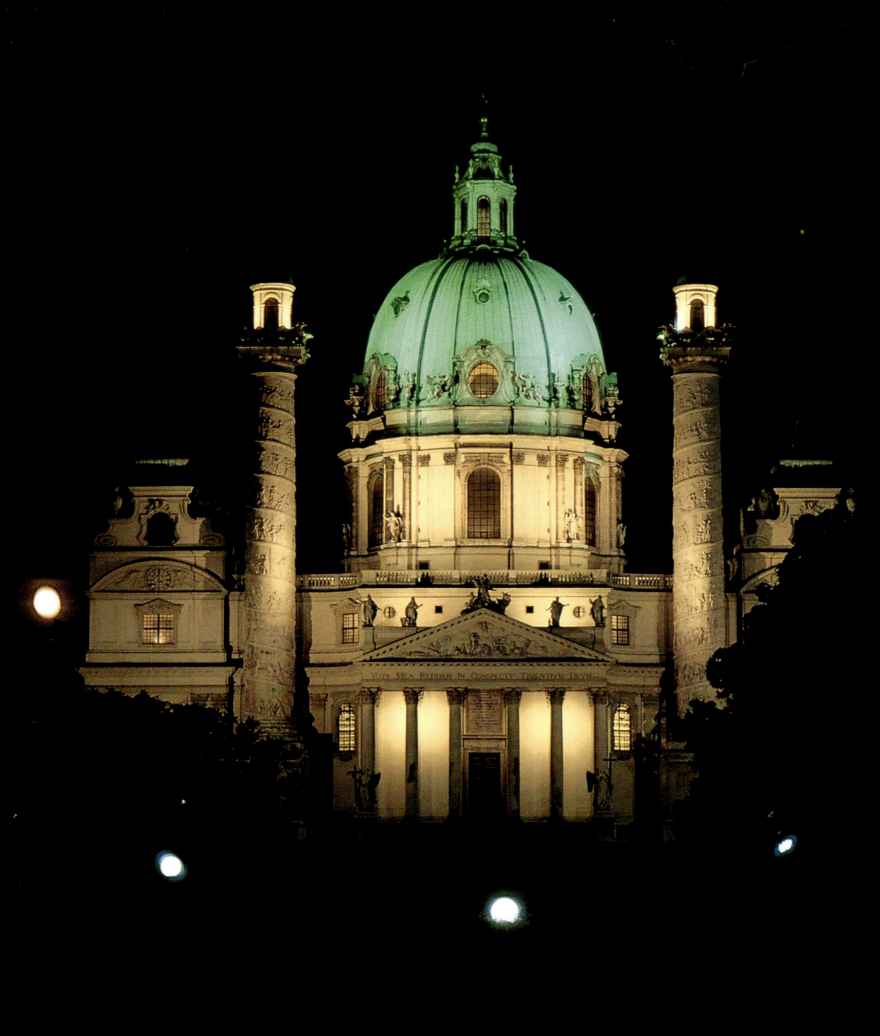

SCHLOSS SCHÖNBRUNN
Rechts: Blick vom Gartenparterre des Parks auf Schloß Schönbrunn (XIII.)

Folgende Doppelseite: Das Palmenhaus im Schloßpark Schönbrunn

SCHÖNBRUNN PALACE
Right: The palace, seen from the lower gardens (XIII District)

Following double page: The Palm House in Schönbrunn Palace Gardens

DENKMÄLER
Links: Mosesbrunnen am Franziskanerplatz, im Hintergrund die Franziskanerkirche

Rechts: Marienstatue auf der Marienbrücke über den Donaukanal

STATUES
Left: Moses Fountain in Franziskanerplatz, with the Franziskanerkirche in the background

Right: Statue of the Virgin Mary on the Marienbrücke, one of the bridges over the Danube Canal

Entlang dem Donaukanal, von der Salztorbrücke bis zur Urania, gibt's den einzigen Versuch einer Wiener Skyline. Vor allem östlich des Kanals – der bald klugerweise in „Kleine Donau" umgetauft wird – zogen Firmen wie Raika, IBM und Bundesländer mächtige Businessbauten auf. Vis-à-vis davon das Textilviertel und Bürohochhäuser wie der trend-profil-Verlag.

Along the Danube Canal, from the Salztorbrücke to the Urania, several attempts have been made at a skyline. Above all on the east side of the canal – which, sensibly enough, is soon to be renamed the Little Danube – companies like Raika, IBM and Bundesländer have erected mighty business edifices. Opposite them is the textile quarter and office blocks such as that of the trend-profil publishing house.

DONAUKANAL UND WIENFLUSS
Links: Blick unter der Aspernbrücke über Schweden- und Marienbrücke auf den Turm der Kirche Maria am Gestade

Folgende Seite (von links oben nach rechts unten): Restaurant-Schiff DDS Johann Strauß am Donaukanal zwischen Marien- und Salztorbrücke; Zollamtssteg über den Wienfluß; Ufer-promenade am Donaukanal; Restaurant-Schiff DDS Johann Strauß

DANUBE CANAL AND WIENFLUSS
Left: View of the spire of Maria am Gestade, seen from under the Aspernbrücke (past the Schwedenbrücke and the Marienbrücke)

Following page (from top left to bottom right): Restaurant ship DDS Johann Strauß on the Danube Canal between Marienbrücke and Salztorbrücke; Zollamtssteg, bridge over the Wienfluß; Embankment promenade along the Danube Canal; Restaurant ship DDS Johann Strauß

DIE DONAU

Rechts: Blick vom Leopoldsberg auf die Donau, mit Nord-, Floridsdorfer-, Nordbahn-, Brigittenauer- und Reichsbrücke

Folgende Doppelseite: Die Neue Donau mit dem Vergnügungszentrum „Copa Cagrana" (XXII.) und Leopoldsberg

THE RIVER DANUBE
Right: View of the Danube from Leopoldsberg, showing the Nordbrücke, the Floridsdorferbrücke, the Nordbahnbrücke, the Brigittenauerbrücke and the Reichsbrücke

Following double page: The New Danube and the Copa Cagrana recreation area (XXII District), with Leopoldsberg in the background

Ah, wie lange ist es eigentlich her, daß die alte Reichsbrücke einstürzte? Damals war die Polizei noch nachsichtig und weich, wenn man in Strebersdorf einen Heurigen gefunden hatte, der bis in den Morgen offenhielt, und dann heimfuhr über die Brücke ins Zentrum, auf ein Frühstück im Café Landtmann oder im Café Kammerspiele.

How long is it now, since the old Reichsbrücke collapsed? At that time the police were still lenient and soft-hearted if one had found a Heurige in Strebersdorf which was open until the early hours of the morning and was then driving back over the bridge to the city centre, to a breakfast in Café Landtmann or Café Kammerspiele.

STRASSENVERKEHR
Rechts (von links oben nach rechts unten): Blick von der Heiligenstädter Lände auf den Turm des Fernheizwerks (IX.); Fußgängerzone in der Favoritenstraße (X.); Opernring von der Babenbergerstraße; Kärntner Ring von der Akademiestraße; Reichsbrücke mit Blick auf den Stephansdom
Folgende Doppelseite: Zeitungsverkäufer unter dem Viadukt der Stadtbahn auf dem Währinger Gürtel/ Nußdorfer Straße
Seite 100 (von links oben nach rechts unten): Lerchenfelder Gürtel mit Stadtbahnstation Josefstädter Straße (VIII.); Stadtbahnstation Stadtpark (III.); Blick vom Franz-Josefs-Kai auf Otto Wagners Schützenhaus am Donaukanal (II.); Triester Straße (X.); Stadtbahnbogen Währinger Gürtel/Nußdorfer Straße in Richtung Döbling (XIX.); Stadtautobahn Südosttangente (X.)

Traffic
Right (from top left to bottom right): Tower of the district heating plant, seen from the Heiligenstädter Lände (IX District); Pedestrian area in Favoritenstraße (X District); The Opernring, seen from Babenbergerstraße; The Kärntnerring, seen from Akademiestraße; The Reichsbrücke, with St. Stephen's in the background
Following double page: Newspaper sellers beneath the Nußdorferstraße viaduct (metropolitan railway)
Page 100 (from top left to bottom right): Josefstädterstraße station (VIII District) Lerchenfeldergürtel; Stadtpark Station (III District); Otto Wagner's Schützenhaus on the Danube Canal (II District), seen from Franz Josefs-Kai; Triester Straße (X District); Nußdorfer Straße viaduct (XIX. District); City highway (X District)

Nacht-Arbeit *Night Work*

Photographen sehen. Da sie sehen, fühlen sie. Wenn sie sehen und fühlen und wie Harry Weber die unendlichen Tücken der Nachtphotographie nachtwandlerisch im Griff haben, dann kommt es zu diesen Bildern einer verwunschenen Welt. Darf man sagen: verwunschen?

Boshaft gesagt: Da des Wieners Glück erst durch das Unglück des Nächsten die höchste Weihe erfährt, empfiehlt sich dem Nachtstreicher ein wacher Blick auf die Arbeitenden.

Es gibt keine glücklichen Nachtarbeiter. Es schaut nur manchmal so aus. Es ist eher eine Welt des Charles Dickens. Der kleine U-Bahn-Kontrollor hat Angst. Der Stadtbahn-Arbeiter hat keinen Sinn für die nokturne Sinnlichkeit von Zügen. Schneeräumer frieren in der Dunkelheit doppelt. Wie oft haben uns alte Standlerinnen auf dem Naschmarkt im Morgengrauen von ihren Sehnsüchten erzählt, angefeuert von einem Weinbrand, den wir als Gentlemen über die Straße getragen hatten, vom *Drechsler* oder der *Gräfin vom Naschmarkt* her. Die Sehnsüchte der Marktstandlerinnen waren jene der Nachtarbeiter in aller Welt: es kommt immer das Tageslicht drin vor, und Wärme und Badehosen oder luftige weiße Kleider mit blauen Tupfen drin.

Oh ja, es gibt auch den glücklichen Wiener Nachtarbeiter. Nur ist das eine andere Welt. Dieser Glückspilz entspricht annähernd dem Klischee, also der Wirklichkeit Wiens. Es ist der Dichter, der Schreiber, der Maler, oder der Musiker, der seine Noten niederschreibt ohne jedes Instrument auf ein Stück Papier, oder der streunende Photograph, zuweilen der Lesende, der zuhause nach zwei Seiten Grass einschläft, in der geeigneten Bar aber die halbe ‚Blechtrommel' frißt.

Die intellektuelle Nächtlichkeit ist nicht das gleiche wie die lähmende Aufstellarbeit der Standlbauer am Brunnenmarkt im 16. Bezirk. Hier das Feuer der Welterschaffung, das Nachschöpfen als Nachfahre des Schöpfers. Dort fremder Auftrag, Zeitdruck und körperliche Zerschlagenheit.

Wäre es denkbar, daß die Kellner oft die Ärmsten der Armen sind? Sie leben ja in engster Symbiose mit Wiens Nachtkunstarbeitern. Sie sind freundlich eingeschlossen in die Denkarbeit und Diskussion. Und doch sagte einer verzagt: „Ab Mitternacht denke ich bei Nietzsche nur mehr, ob der auch dicke Füße hatte wie ich."

Und wie es den Schönheiten in den Ledherminis geht, die ewige Nachtschicht haben, das weiß keiner außer ihnen. Die Fröhlichkeit oder Tristesse der Nachtarbeit auf dem Gürtel und in den anderen Rotlichtbezirken werten nur jene, die nie damit in Berührung kamen. Webers Bilder interpretieren nichts, wie angenehm. Sie sind unaufdringliche Zuneigung mit Lichtern und Schatten.

Photographers see. Since they see, they feel. When they see and feel and, like Harry Weber, also have an instinctive grasp of the endless tricks of night photography, then the result is these pictures of an enchanted world. Yet is it permissible to say 'enchanted'?

To put it spitefully: since the greatest happiness of the Viennese consists solely in the unhappiness of his or her neighbour, the nighthawk is recommended to cast a wakeful eye at those who have to work at night.

There are no happy night-workers. It only seems as if there are, sometimes. It is, rather, a Dickensian world. The little U-Bahn inspector is afraid. The worker on the metropolitan railway has no sense of the nocturnal sensuousness of the trains; snow-shovellers freeze twice as much in the dark. How often, at daybreak, have old ladies with market stalls in the Naschmarkt told us about their secret longings, fired by a brandy which we, as gentlemen, have carried across the street for them from Drechsler *or the* Gräfin von Naschmarkt. *The longings of the market stallholders were always the same as those of the night-workers all over the world: daylight always figures in them, and warmth and swimming costumes, or airy white dresses with blue polka-dots.*

But there is, nevertheless, also a happy Viennese night-worker. Yet his is another world. This happy fellow roughly corresponds to a cliché, i.e. to Viennese reality. He is a poet, a writer, a painter; or a musician, who writes his music on scraps of paper, without any instrument; or a roaming photographer, or even a reader who falls asleep at home after a page of Günter Grass, *yet devours half the* Tin Drum *in a suitable bar.*

Intellectual night-work is not the same as the crippling work of the stallholders putting up their market stands at the Brunnenmarkt in the 16th District. In the first case, there is the fire of world-creation, the work of reproduction as a descendant of the creator. In the second case, there are instructions from someone else, pressure of work and physical exhaustion.

Is it conceivable that waiters are often the poorest of the poor? After all, they live in the closest symbiosis with Vienna's artistic night-workers. They are amicably included in the work of thinking and in the discussions. And yet one of them said, despondently: "After midnight, all Nietzsche makes me think of is whether he had swollen feet like me."

And just how do those beauties in leather mini-skirts fare, who have an eternal night-shift? That is something which nobody knows but them. The joys or sorrows of night-work on the Gürtel and in the other red-light Districts is only ever evaluated by people who have never come into contact with it. Weber's photographs do not interpret anything at all – how nice! They are unobtrusive affection with lights and shadows.

Nachtwache vor der Radetzkykaserne (XV.).
Night watch in front of the Radetzky Barracks (XV District)

101

SPÄTE ZUGS-
VERBINDUNGEN
Links (von oben nach unten): Bahnhof Hütteldorf (XIV.); Westbahnhof (XV.); Bahnhof Hütteldorf

Rechts: Westbahnhof

CATCHING THE LAST TRAIN
Left (from top to bottom): Hütteldorf station (XIV District); Westbahnhof (XV District); Hütteldorf station (XIV District)

Right: Westbahnhof

Es gibt feine Pinkel, die immer reich waren und arm blieben, weil sie vieles nicht mitbekamen. Beispielsweise den nächtlichen und frühmorgendlichen Zauber der Bahnhöfe Wiens. Die Szene ist sozial im Keller angesiedelt, doch Überraschungen sind beinah vorprogrammiert. Aus dem dunklen Ozean der heiligen Trinker und tatsächlich rettungslos verlorenen Seelen, die nicht mehr aus dem Inländer-Rum in die Wirklichkeit finden, blitzen die Leuchtfeuer witziger Genies und philosophischer Aussteiger. Dort ist die Welt der schärfsten Weisheiten zu Hause, geschliffen von einem Leben am Abgrund.

There are those 'Lord Mucks' who were always rich and yet have remained poor because they have never known anything else. For example, the magic of Vienna's railway stations in the night and early morning. Socially, the scene is located at basement level, yet surprises are almost preordained. The beacons of humourous geniuses and philosophical drop-outs flash from the dark ocean of holy drinkers and those truly and irredeemably lost souls who no longer find their way back to reality from Inländer Rum. *This is a world where the keenest wisdom is at home, sharpened from life on the edge of the abyss.*

NACHTVERKEHR
Links: U-Bahn-Station Hütteldorf (XIV.)

Rechts (von links oben nach rechts unten): Straßenbahn-Remise in Favoriten (X.); Gastarbeiter-Autobus vor dem Südbahnhof (X.); Impressionen vom nächtlichen Südbahnhof; Schalterhalle des Südbahnhofs; Nachtzug im Bahnhof Hütteldorf

TRAFFIC AT NIGHT
Left: Hütteldorf U-Bahn station (XIV District)

Right (from top left to bottom right): Tramshed (X District); Gastarbeiter *bus taking foreign workers to Südbahnhof (X District); Impressions of Südbahnhof by night; Südbahnhof, booking hall; Night train at Hütteldorf station*

Warum diese Ballung müder Seelen auf Bahnhöfen? Die Antwort hat drei Teile. Dort kommt man eben ausgelaugt an. Und es ist warm dort. Und die abfahrenden Züge geben die Illusion, man könne jederzeit weg in ein lächelndes Land voll Sonne. Den Ärmsten gelten selbst Straßenbahn und U-Bahn als Verheißung einer schönen Flucht.

Why is there this mass of tired souls at the station? There are three parts to the answer. One arrives there exhausted. And it is warm there. And the departing trains give rise to the illusion that one could at any time leave for a smiling country full of sunshine. For the poorest of the poor, even the trams and the underground represent the promise of a beautiful escape.

NASCHMARKT
Links und rechts:
Frühschicht auf den
Naschmarkt-Ständen
(IV. und VI.)

*NASCHMARKT AT NIGHT
Early morning shift
at the Naschmarkt
(IV and VI District)*

Wie gerne würde man Studenten der Wirtschafts-Uni und der Technischen Universität wünschen, sie würden wie in alten Zeiten mit Saft und Kraft eine Wiener Nacht lang durchdiskutieren und sich dann, im Morgengrauen, auf den Naschmarkt verfügen. Hier winkt ein zweites Studium. Hier gäbe es ein Eintauchen ins Diluvium der Handelswissenschaften, in die Steinzeit der Hi-Tech – und in die Psychologie des ältesten, nie aus der Mode gekommenen Verkaufsschmähs. Der Naschmarkt ist ein Kontinent für sich. Die umliegenden Lokale sind wie Hafenstädte, haben praktisch nie geschlossen. Mit Zuneigung erwähnen wir den eleganten Herrn Drechsler, dessen Café ein Hort der Sicherheit ist.

How one wishes that, as in the old days, the students at the Commercial University and the Technical University would carry on vigorous discussions all through the Viennese night and then, in the first light of dawn, proceed to the Naschmarkt. Here, a second course of studies would beckon them. Here, they would be immersed in the diluvial age of the commercial sciences, in the stone age of high tech, and in the psychology of the oldest sales jokes there are - ones which never go out of fashion. The Naschmarkt is a continent in itself. The surrounding pubs and restaurants are like seaports, they practically never close. We mention with affection the elegant Herr Drechsler, whose café is a hearth of security.

FLOHMARKT
Links und rechts:
„Antiquitäten"-Händler
auf dem Flohmarkt
(V. und VI.)

FLEA MARKET AT NIGHT
'Antique' dealers at the
Flea Market
(V and VI District)

Wir gehen im Text selten direkt auf die Photos ein. Doch eine der Ausnahmen muß das Bild zur Linken sein. So wie man einen neuen Roman von Saul Bellow zuvor in der Hand wiegen und beschnüffeln sollte, ehe man ihn liest, sollte man dieses Bild Millimeter für Millimeter wägen und ins Herz versenken. Wir sehen die eigentlich schönste Frau der Welt, nicht mehr ganz jung, gewiß kein leichtes Leben hinter und keine Villen-Existenz vor sich, doch eine erhebende Erscheinung, gekrönt von einem wissenden, zur Gerechtigkeit neigenden Blick, die Kleidung rundum nicht mit der zitternden Hand der Eitlen gewählt, sondern mit dem Willen und der Vorstellungskraft eines umfassend pragmatischen Geistes.
Wir befinden uns hier übrigens auf dem Flohmarkt. Der ist in Wien immer auch Casino. Unter sensationellem Klumpert finden sich ab und an halt doch ein Original des Rudolf von Alt, ein unerkanntes Spezialmöbel von Thonet oder ein Glas von Koloman Moser, das den Kenner, der seufzend 50 Schilling gibt, um die nächste Ecke zu einem glücklich schluchzenden Bürger macht.

In the commentary we seldom go into the photographs directly. Yet an exception has to be the picture on the left. Just as one should first weigh a new novel by Saul Bellow in one's hand and sniff it a bit before reading it, so one should ponder this photograph millimetre for millimetre and let it sink into one's heart. What we actually see is the most beautiful woman in the world. No longer so young, she certainly has no easy life behind her and no villa-existence before her, yet she is a woman of exalting appearance, crowned by a knowing look which inclines toward justice; her whole wardrobe is chosen not with the trembling hand of the vain, but with the will and imagination of a comprehensively pragmatic spirit.
Incidentally, we are here at the Flea Market. In Vienna, this is always also a casino. Among sensational rubbish, one now and then happens to find an original by Rudolf von Alt, a special piece of Thonet furniture which has gone unrecognised or a glass by Koloman Moser. The connoisseur who pays his 50 Schillings with a sigh then sobs with delight as soon as he turns the first corner.

BEIM KLEINEN SACHER
Rechts (von links oben nach rechts unten): Würstelstand zwischen Naglergasse und dem Platz Am Hof (großes Bild und kleines Bild oben); Maronibraterin am Christkindlmarkt am Rathausplatz; Opernballbesucher beim Würstelstand am Albertinaplatz

AT THE SAUSAGE STAND (known as the 'kleine Sacher')
Right (from top left to bottom right): Sausage stand between Naglergasse and Am Hof (large picture and small picture top right); Woman selling roasted chestnuts at the Christmas fair in Rathausplatz; Guests from the Opera Ball at the sausage stand in the Albertinaplatz

NACHTVERKEHR
Links: Rotlicht-Bezirk am Gürtel (großes Bild), beim Westbahnhof (XV.) und in der Mollardgasse (VI.)

Folgende Seite: Nachtdienst der Polizei in der Seitenstettengasse

*STREET LIFE
Left: Red light district on the Gürtel (large picture) near Westbahnhof (XV District) and in Mollardgasse (VI District)*

Following page: Policeman on night shift in Seitenstettengasse

Wo Wiens Arbeits-Szene wirklich international ist: In der UNO-City bei Tag und den teils hübschen, teils trübseligen Rotlichtbezirken bei Nacht. Im hingebungsvollsten Wirtschaftszweig gibt es entzükkende babylonische Sprachverwirrungen, mit starken Färbungen ins Osteuropäische und Asiatische.

Where Vienna's working scene really is international: in the UNO city by day, and in the red-light Districts – at times pretty, at times depressing – by night. In the most devoted of all business sectors there is a delightfully Babylonian confusion of tongues, with distinct eastern European and Asiatic colourings.

113

Nacht-Plaisir *Night Pleasure*

Arbeiten wir uns bei diesem Thema von unten nach oben, vom Horizontalen ins Vertikale. Gehen wir getrost davon aus, daß „Nachtleben" zuerst mit dem klassischen „Nachtlokal" verbunden wird, nicht mit abendlichem Orgelspiel in der Michaelerkirche.

Die Lokale mit dem bunten Neonblinzeln heißen überall auf der Welt gleich. Auch Wien hat sein „Chez Nous", seine „Moulin Rouge". Sie sind kaufmännisch schwer einzuschätzen. Sind sie Weihestätten des Reichtums? Krachen sie wie die Kaisersemmeln? Ist Wien bei Nacht in Schwung oder am Sand? Die Steuerbehörden wüßten das ebenfalls gern, doch Ratlosigkeit selbst dort. Es kann nicht ganz verkehrt sein, die Nachtclubs und Separée-Tempel als internationalen Durchschnitt einzustufen. Es fehlt der geschichtliche Ruf von Paris, die reiche Klientel von London, die betäubende Exotik etwa der Wanchai in Hongkong oder der Copacabana. Gottlob fehlt auch die humorlose Direktheit Hamburgs. Wien bietet, von den Nachtschönheiten her, Witz und Würde einer Völkermischung, es ist alles da von hoher Eleganz bis zu tiefster Provinz.

Homosexuelle Globetrotter beklagen ein kümmerliches Niveau, man spiele hier nicht in der gleichen Liga wie New York, von San Franzisko ganz zu schweigen. Und wie geht es eleganten Geschäftsfrauen, die nach den Niederungen des Tages einen Berg von Begleiter suchen? Hoffentlich besser, als wir es mit unserer bescheidenen Erfahrung vermuten.

Wenden wir uns vom Zwinker-Neon ins Stakkato-Neon der jungen Discos. Die oszillieren werdend-sterbend-werdend wie die Top-Bands und Pop-Stars auf ihren Plattentellern. Dem flackernden Disco-Pfad folgt der sportliche Trinker am besten mit Hilfe des „Falter" – jener erstklassigen Stadtzeitung, die gerade den nächtlichen Essern und Trinkern, den Traurigen und Tänzern, den Lüstlingen und Lumpen ein Licht in der Finsternis ist.

Natürlich gehört auch vieles andere zum Nachtplaisir der Metropole: Noble Restaurants, selige Heurige, literarisch anmutende Cafés. Das sind elementare Bausteine Wiens – wir haben sie als Fundament im Prolog gerühmt.

Verweisen wir noch hastig und glücklich auf das Bermuda-Dreieck, eine strahlende Fülle eng geschachtelter Lokale zwischen dem Hohen Markt und dem Kai. Toll für Virile allen Alters, schön für die großäugigen Fremden. Endlich hat auch Wien das Grundgesetz des nachbarschaftlichen Wettbewerbs und des Nachtgeschäfts begriffen: „Menschen gehen am Abend dorthin, wo sich der Himmel rot färbt, weil darunter die Hölle los ist."

In einem Wiener Innenstadt-Lokal
A restaurant in Vienna's inner city

In dealing with this theme, let us work our way from the bottom to the top, from the horizontal to the vertical. Let us begin with the fact that, first and foremost, 'night-life' is connected with the classic 'night-club' and not with an evening organ recital in the Michaelerkirche.

The clubs with colourful, winking neon-lights bear the same names all the world over. Vienna, too, has its Chez Nous, its Moulin Rouge. They are difficult to classify commercially. Are they shrines to wealth? Do they crack like Kaisersemmeln? *Is Vienna-by-Night booming or bust? The tax authorities would also like to know the answer to that, yet even they are in a state of perplexity. One cannot be wrong in classifying the night-clubs and séparée-temples as internationally average in standard. They lack the historical reputation of Paris, the wealthy clientele of London, the stunning exoticism of Wanchai in Hong Kong, or of the Copacabana. They also – thank God! – lack the humourless straightforwardness of Hamburg. As far as examples of nocturnal beauty are concerned, Vienna offers the wit and dignity of a mixture of peoples; everything is there, from great elegance to the deepest provinciality.*

Homosexual globetrotters complain of a pitiful standard; here, one is not in the same league as New York, not to mention San Francisco. And how do elegant businesswomen fare when, after the dumps of the day, they search for masses of escorts? Hopefully better than we surmise from our own modest experience.

Let us turn from the winking neon-lights to the staccato neon of the young discos. These oscillate, becoming-dying-and-becoming like the top bands and pop stars on their turntables. The sportmanslike drinker follows the flickering path of the disco at best with the help of Falter, *that first-rate city magazine which is a light in the darkness, especially for nocturnal eaters and drinkers, for those who feel depressed and those who want to dance, for sensualists and scoundrels.*

Of course, there are also many other sides to the nocturnal pleasure of the metropolis. High-class restaurants, delightful Heurige, *cafés with literary pretensions. They are the elementary building blocks of Vienna – their fundamental role has already been eulogised in the prologue.*

Let us hastily and happily refer the reader to the Bermuda Triangle, a glorious plethora of closely nested pubs between the Hohen Markt and the Kai. Great for virile people of all ages, beautiful to wide-eyed foreigners. At last Vienna, too, has understood the fundamental law of neighbourly competition and nocturnal business: "In the evenings, people go where the sky turns red, because there below all hell is loose."

DAS WIENER KAFFEE-
HAUS
Links: Café Alt Wien
(I. Bäckerstraße)
Rechts: Café Hawelka
(I. Dorotheergasse)

Folgende Seite (von
links oben nach rechts
unten): Kleines Wiener
Café (VIII. Kochgasse);
Kleines Café
(I. Franziskanerplatz);
Café Frauenhuber
(I. Himmelpfortgasse)

*THE VIENNESE COFFEE
HOUSE
Left: Café Alt Wien
(Bäckerstraße,
I District)
Right: Café Hawelka
(Dorotheergasse,
I District)*

*Following page (from
top left to bottom
right): Kleines Wiener
Café (Kochgasse,
VIII District);
Kleines Café
(Franziskanerplatz,
I District); Café
Frauenhuber (Himmel-
pfortgasse, I District)*

Das Hawelka hat, da es nie modernisierte, alles überstanden, sogar die zahllosen Lobpreisungen, oder die männlichen Kellner, die häufig unter Menstruationsbeschwerden zu leiden scheinen, oder die Danzer-Frage „Wos mocht a Nockata im Hawelka?". Was machen eigentlich die Künstler? Sie kommen noch, aber heute ist es schon gut, wenn zur selben Zeit der Dramatiker Heinz R. Unger da sitzt, und sein Freund Lui Dimanche, und Kunstkenner wie Ex-Galeriebesitzer Allmayer-Beck oder Kurt Kalb. Das Schönste an diesem Café: Es ist eine Wohnung geblieben, und kein entzückenderer Anblick, als wenn die Frau Hawelka an ihrem Tischerl listig die Groscherln zählt, als nahe das Ende der Welt.

Since it has never been modernised, Hawelka has survived everything, even the innumberable eulogies, the male waiters who frequently seem to suffer from menstrual complaints, and the question in the Georg Danzer song: "What's a nude doing in Hawelka?". Where are the artists, anyway? They still come here, but today one is lucky to find the dramatist Heinz R. Unger sitting there at the same time as his friend, Lui Dimanche, or art connoisseurs such as the former gallery owners Allmayer-Beck and Kurt Kalb. The best thing about this café is that it has remained a living-room, and there is no sight more charming than that of Frau Hawelka slyly counting the takings at her little table, as if the end of the world were nigh.

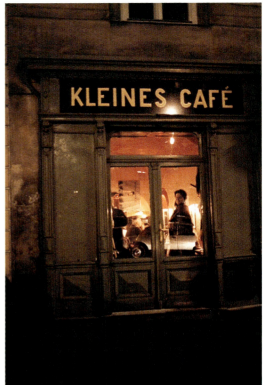

Wien hat so eine große Liebe fürs Kleine: Kleiner Mocca, kleines Pantscherl, Kleines Wiener Café, Kleines Café. In letzterem ist Mime Hanno Pöschl zuhaus. Er wollte sich mit Radfahren verkleinern. Seitdem nahm er 10 Kilo zu. Ein Wiener Schicksal, ein kleines.

Vienna has such a big heart for what is small: a small mocca, a little bit of a flirt, the Kleines Wiener Café, the Kleines Café. The mime Hanno Pöschl is at home in the last-mentioned. He recently wanted to reduce his own size by cycling. Since then he has put on 10 kilogrammes. A Viennese fate, a minor one.

DER WIENER HEURIGE
Rechts: Mayer am Pfarrplatz in Heiligenstadt (XIX.)

*AT THE VIENNESE HEURIGEN
Right: Mayer am Pfarrplatz (Heiligenstadt, XIX District)*

Am schönsten sind natürlich die kleinen, billigen, eher stillen Heurigenlokale, die kein Bus findet. Dort können auch die Pensionisten ihr tausendmal verdientes Viertel trinken, ohne zu verarmen. Manche Schickimicki-Heurige, deren Klientel den Intelligenzquotienten einer Nudelsuppe hat, nähern sich in den Preisen dem heurigen Ritz-Niveau.

Best of all, of course, are those Heurigen, or wine taverns, which are small, cheap, rather quiet, and cannot be reached by bus. There, even pensioners can drink that quart of wine which they have earned a thousand times over, without becoming impoverished. Some of the trendy Heurige, whose clientele has about the IQ of noodle soup, have prices approaching the present-day Ritz level.

DER WIENER HEURIGE
Links: In den Weinbergen von Salmannsdorf (XIX.)

Rechts (von links oben nach rechts unten): Heurigenschenken in Neustift, Grinzing, Nußdorf und Ottakring (rechts unten: Die Volkssängerin Anni Demuth im Heurigen „Zum alten Drahrer" im Liebhartstal)

AT THE VIENNESE HEURIGEN
Left: In the vineyards of Salmannsdorf (XIX District)

Right (from top left to bottom right): Wine taverns in Neustift, Grinzing, Nußdorf and Ottakring (below right: popular Heurigen singer Anni Demuth at an Ottakringer Heurigen, Zum alten Drahrer, Liebhartstal, XVI District)

Der Heurige! Ein Wort, das keine Mehrzahl kennt. Die Heurigen sind nämlich Erdäpfel. Es gibt ohnehin keine zwei gleichen Lokale dieser Rasse. Beliebte Recherche einsamer Durstiger: wieviele Arten gibt es? Pro Wiener Nacht gehen sich zirka acht aus. Heinz Holecek, unser großer Kammersänger, Erzähler und Wissensdurstiger hat einmal mitgezählt.

The Heurige! A word which knows only the singular. The plural (Heurigen) means, namely, potatoes. At any rate, no two wine taverns of this kind are the same. The favourite research undertaken by thirsty solitaries: how many different kinds are there? Approximately eight of them can be fitted into one Viennese night. Heinz Holecek, our great Kammersänger and storyteller, and a man with a thirst for knowledge, once counted them.

DER WIENER PRATER
Links und rechts: Impressionen aus dem Wurstelprater

Folgende Doppelseite: Das Riesenrad vom Praterstern (II.)

Seiten 126/127: Autodrome und Hochschaubahnen im Wurstelprater

THE PRATER
Left and right: Impressions from the Wurstelprater *fun-fair*

Following double page: The giant Ferris wheel, seen from Praterstern (II District)

126 – 127: Dodgems and the big dipper at the Wurstelprater

Calafati. Die dickste Frau. Der stärkste Mann. Die längste Schlange. Die schnellsten Go-Carts. Die verknofeltsten Langos. Luftdruckgewehr und rote Rose. Und natürlich das Riesenrad. Diese superlative Welt empfiehlt sich dem Nachtreisenden, der sich günstig das Kindliche bewahrt – oder grade ein Nachtkind hofiert.

Calafati. The fattest woman. The strongest man. The longest snake. The fastest go-carts. The most garlicky langos. An air rifle and a red rose. And of course the giant Ferris wheel. This world of superlatives can be recommended to the night traveller who is lucky enough to have preserved the child within – or happens to be courting a child of the night.

SZENELOKALE, BEISELN UND RESTAURANTS
Links (von links oben nach rechts unten): Oswald & Kalb (I. Bäckerstraße); Erste Wiener Gasthof-Brauerei (XIX. Billrothstraße); Café Drechsler am Naschmarkt (VI. Linke Wienzeile); Do & Co im Haas-Haus (I. Stephansplatz); Kleines Café (I. Franziskanerplatz); Crêperie Brasserie Spittelberg (VII. Gutenberggasse)
Rechts: Zum Basilisken (I. Schönlaterngasse)

PUBS, INNS AND RESTAURANTS
Left (from top right to bottom left): Oswald & Kalb (Bäckerstraße, I District); Erste Wiener Gasthof-Brauerei (Billrothstraße, XIX District), Café Drechsler (am Naschmarkt, Linke Wienzeile, VI District); Do & Co in the Haas-Haus (St. Stephen's Square, I District); Kleines Café (Franziskanerplatz, I District); Creperie Brasserie Spittelberg (Gutenberggasse, VII District)
Right: Zum Basilisken (Schönlaterngasse, VII District)

Der Attila Dogudan, der mit seinem Do & Co im Haas-Haus auf diesen Seiten vorkommt, hat fein abgehoben, auch als Bordverpfleger von Nikis Lauda-Air. Die andern Szenelokale tragen teils jung & billig zum wichtigsten geistigen Umweltschutz bei: selber reden am Abend statt fernsehen.

Attila Dogudan, who appears on these pages with his Do & Co in Haas-Haus, has really taken off, among other things as the flight caterer for Niki's Lauda Air. Other in-pubs, with a younger and less exclusive clientele, make an important contribution towards the protection of the mental environment by encouraging people, to do their own talking in the evenings instead of watching television.

IM BERMUDA-
DREIECK
Links: Krah, Krah
(I. Rabensteig)

Rechts (von oben nach
unten): Roter Engel
(I. Rabensteig); Krah,
Krah; Ma Pitom
(I. Seitenstettengasse)

THE BERMUDA
TRIANGLE
Left: Krah-Krah
(Rabensteig, I District)

Right (from top to
bottom): Roter Engel
(Rabensteig, I District);
Krah-Krah; Ma Pitom
(Seitenstettengasse,
I District)

Seit Stefan Zweigs „Sternstunden der Menschheit"
wissen wir: Geschichte wird von einzelnen
gemacht. Das gilt auch für die Lokalszene Wien.
Ein extrem kreativer Muskel ist Michael Satke. Er
schuf die „Reiss-Bar" und den „Roten Engel". Ein
anderer Lokalgestalter ist hauptberuflich Kunst-
händler: Kurt, der goldene Kalb. Ein Midas, dem
die Wirtshäuser, in die er seine Finger steckte,
zum Erfolg wurden: Oswald & Kalb, Café
Salzgries, angeblich auch Café Engländer.
Freilich ist auch das Bewahren eine Kunst. Da
muß der Kommerzialrätin Elfriede Gabriel die
Krone aufgesetzt werden, mit der „Bonbonniere"
in der Spiegelgasse. Hier fühlen sich seit Jahr-
zehnten die Arrivierten wohl, beispielsweise auch
Kalb und Satke.

Stefan Zweig's Sternstunden der Menschheit *('The
Tide of Fortune') teaches us that history is made by
individuals. That goes for Vienna's pub scene too.
One man with a lot of creative muscle is Michael
Satke. He created the Reiss-Bar and the Roter
Engel. Another pub-designer is an art dealer by
profession: Kurt 'the golden calf' Kalb. A man with
the Midas touch, all the pubs in which he has a
finger turn into succeses: Oswald & Kalb, Café
Salzgries, and, allegedly, Café Engländer as well.
Of course, preservation is also an art. The crown
for that has to go to a Counsellor of Commerce,
Elfriede Gabriel, for her Bonbonniere, in the
Spiegelgasse. Successful people – including Kalb
and Satke, for example – have felt at home there
for decades.*

SZENELOKALE, BEISELN UND RESTAURANTS
Links (von links oben nach rechts unten): Bane (I. Köllnerhofgasse); Aera (I. Gonzagagasse); Erste Wiener Gasthof-Brauerei (XIX.); Kaktus (I. Seitenstettengasse); Salettl (XIX. Hartäckerstraße); Café Alt Wien (I. Bäckerstraße); Bane (I. Köllnerhofgasse); Kix Bar (I. Bäckerstraße); Krah, Krah (I. Rabensteig)
Rechts: Aera

PUBS, INNS AND RESTAURANTS
Left (from top left to bottom right): Bane (Köllnerhofgasse, I District); Aera (Gonzagagasse, I District); Erste Wiener Gasthof Brauerei (XIX. District); Kaktus (Seitenstettengasse, I District); "Salettl" (Hartäckerstraße, District); Café Alt Wien (Bäckerstraße, I District); Bane (Köllnerhofgasse, I District); Kix Bar (Bäckerstraße, I District); Krah-Krah (Rabensteig, I District)
Right: Aera

Die Seitenstettengasse ist was Wunderbares. Sie ist das Herzstück des Bermudadreiecks, liegt genau zwischen dem ältesten Christenbau von Wien, der Ruprechtskirche, und dem Tempel der jüdischen Gemeinde. Die Tempelwächter mit Maschinenpistolen geben der ausgelassenen Gasse ein kühnes G'schau. Der Nachtschwärmer hat eine verwirrende Auswahl, muß sich halt durchbeißen von „Rasputin" über „Kuchldragoner", „Kaktus", „Ma Pitom" bis zum „Krah Krah". Bemerkenswertes City-Pendant zu dieser Gasse: Judenplatz plus Kurrentgasse, dominiert durch die drei Lokale des Kontaktgenies Celestino Conte, unweit davon „Ofenloch", „Treff", "Push In", „Zum Scherer" und Bürgermeisters Lieblingswirt Gustl „Bauer".

The Seitenstettengasse is something marvellous. It is the heart of the Bermuda Triangle, situated exactly halfway between the oldest Christian building in Vienna, the Ruprechtskirche, and the temple of the Jewish community. The temple guards with their machine-guns give the lively street a bold appearance. The nighthawk is confronted by a bewildering choice and has to bite his way through from Rasputin, Kuchldragoner, Kaktus and Ma Pitom down to Krah Krah.
Worth noting is the companion piece to this street, also in the city centre: Judenplatz plus Kurrentgasse, dominated by the three pubs of the contact genius Celestino Conte, not far from which are Ofenloch, Treff, Push In, Zum Scherer and the Mayor's favourite pub, Gustl Bauer.

DISCOS UND MUSIK-
LOKALE
Links und rechts:
Disco Nachtwerk
(XXIII. Dr. Gonda-
Gasse)

Folgende Seite (von
links oben nach rechts
unten): Atrium (IV.
Schwarzenbergplatz);
Nachtwerk; Zugabe
(IV. Schwarzenberg-
platz); Silvester-
Musikfest in einem
Zelt am Platz Am Hof;
Jazzland (I. Franz-
Josefs-Kai); Atrium

*DISCOS AND MUSIC
PUBS
Left and right: Disco
Nachtwerk (Dr. Gonda-
Gasse, XXIII District)*

*Following page (from
top left to bottom
right): Atrium
(Schwarzenbergplatz,
VI District); Nachtwerk;
Zugabe (Schwarzen-
bergplatz, VI District);
New Year music
festival in a tent in Am
Hof; Jazzland (Franz
Josefs-Kai, I District);
Atrium*

Viele Österreicher, verdorben durch die Drolerie
„Märchenprinz" der „Ersten Allgemeinen
Verunsicherung", glauben die Discos fest in
Provinzhand. Das stimmt nicht. Man steht in Wien
ziemlich oft ziemlich lang vor einer Disco auf der
Straße, bis wieder Platz ist – es sei denn, man
kommt gleich als *big spender* durch die Gesichts-
kontrolle.
Walter, unser kunstsinniger, der Homophilie
verpflichteter Freund, ergänzt: „Die Discos
können sich wirklich sehen lassen. Aber wirklich
gut, von der Kleidung und auch von der Musik
her, wird's natürlich erst an einem für *Gays*
reservierten Abend. Ihr Fehlgeleiteten habt keine
Ahnung, was Euch entgeht."

*Many Austrians, corrupted by the drollery of the
song* Märchenprinz, *by the rock band* Erste
Allgemeine Verunsicherung, *think that discos are
all very provincial. That is not true. In Vienna, one
often has to wait quite a long time on the street
outside a disco, until there is once again enough
room inside unless, of course, you get through the
face check immediately as a 'big spender'.
Walter, a committed homophile friend of ours, with
good artistic taste, adds: "The discos are certainly
worth seeing. But it only gets really good, as far as
the clothes and also the music are concerned, at an
evening reserved for gays. All you poor misguided
people don't have a clue what you're missing."*

Wir haben unsere Hetz damit, den jazzenden Freunden Heinz Neubrand, Klavier, und Alexander Späth, Kontrabaß, in verschiedenen Lokalen zu lauschen. Dennoch: könnte in dieser Welthauptstadt der Musik nicht mehr Jazz sein, mehr Mississippi in der Donau? Striptease ist ja auf die Dauer nicht abendfüllend und für die Ohrwaschln ganz schlecht.

We get our fun listening to the two jazz friends, Heinz Neubrand, piano, and Alexander Späth, double-bass, when they play in various pubs in Vienna. Nevertheless, here in the world capital of music, couldn't there be a bit more jazz, a bit more Mississippi in the Danube? After all, in the long run, you cannot fill up every evening with a striptease show – which, anyway, is very bad for your ears.

BARS UND NIGHTCLUBS
Rechts: Moulin Rouge (I. Walfischgasse)

Folgende Doppelseite (von links oben nach rechts unten): Moulin Rouge (großes Bild); Broadway Piano-Bar (I. Bauernmarkt); Eden-Bar (I. Liliengasse); Moulin Rouge

*BARS AND NIGHTCLUBS
Right: Moulin Rouge (Walfischgasse, I District)*

Following double page (from top left to bottom right): Moulin Rouge (large picture); Broadway Piano Bar (Bauernmarkt, I District); Eden-Bar (Liliengasse, I District); Moulin Rouge

Zwei weitere Leuchttürme in der Nacht: Bela Koreny, wunderbarer Künstler, Wirt und Mensch mit seiner „Broadway"-Bar. Heinz Werner Schimanko, extrem bunte Schale mit Rolls Royce, Harley, 110 Kilo, Vollglatze, darunter ein moderner, hochintelligenter Unternehmer, verantwortlich u. a. für Prominentenbar Eden, Moulin Rouge und das merkwürdige Hotel Orient.

Two further lighthouses in the night: Bela Koreny, a great artist, publican and human being, with his Broadway Bar. Heinz Werner Schimanko, an extremely colourful exterior with Rolls-Royce, Harley, 110 kilogrammes, and bald head; among other things a modern, highly intelligent businessman, he is responsible for e.g. the celebrity bar Eden, the Moulin Rouge and the remarkable Hotel Orient.

Sperrstunde
Oben (von oben nach unten): Café Bräunerhof (I. Stallburggasse);
Café Europa (I. Kärntnerstraße); Café Konditorei Aida (XX.)

Closing Time
From top to bottom: Café Bräunerhof (Stallburggasse, I District); Café Europa (Kärntner Straße, I District); Café-Konditorei Aida (XX District)

„Sperrstund is" – Hans Mosers schönstes und traurigstes Lied

"Sperrstund is" ('Time gentlemen, please') – Hans Moser's most beautiful, most melancholy song.

Epilog *Epilogue*

Die Autoren des Buches, der Photograph wie der Texter, waren lange Zeit umnachtet. Wir liebten das finstere Wien über alles. Viele Jahre lang schwebten wir darin wie Glühwürmchen. Wir waren eher stille Gäste der Nacht. Den einen sah man oft mit der Kamera, den anderen mit der Füllfeder. Wir hatten unseren fairen Anteil an Streitgesprächen, aber keine Raufhändel. Jedenfalls wurden wir niemals verhaftet. Gleichwohl kennen wir viele Polizisten und einige Geheimdienstleute, die argwöhnisch den Weg unseres nächtlichen Fleißes kreuzten.

II.

Heute gehen wir behutsamer mit unserer Kondition um. Wir haben nun auch den frühen Morgen als Stunde der Kreativität entdeckt. Gelegentlich achten wir sogar eine ländliche Gegend. Wir wurden aber weder Verräter noch Konvertiten. Von Zeit zu Zeit tauchen wir noch behutsam ein in die Schönheit der Wiener Nacht, die uns so lang eine Liebe war.

„What's seldom is beautiful", sagen die Briten. Die seltener gewordenen Ausflüge sind besonders schön. Es fehlt ihnen das Inflationäre jener Zeit, als wir die *tägliche Nacht* erfanden. Ihr verdankten wir kleine gesundheitliche Niederlagen und große Siege des schöpferischen Wirkens – oder das, was zunächst danach aussah, bei Tageslicht aber manchmal wie eine Seifenblase zerfiel. Die Gesamtbilanz blieb überwältigend positiv. Wir waren emsig und angeregt, durchaus erhoben durch einen *Genius loci* der nächtlichen alten Stadt.

III.

Wobei „alte Stadt" nur mehr im besten Sinne gilt: Für die Bausubstanz, die Geschichtstiefe, die großen Linien der stadttechnischen Architektur, das friedlich-schlamperte Ineinanderkämmen der grünen Außenbezirke mit dem Kern der City, an unscharfen Binnengrenzen voller Überraschungen.

Abgesehen von diesen Grundwerten darf auch von einer neuen Stadt gesprochen werden. Der „Falter", die ausgezeichnete, zuverlässige Stadtzeitung, manchmal rabiat-rauhbeinig im Zurichten prominenter Opfer, meist aber auf der Suche nach intelligenter Gerechtigkeit, verzeichnet allmonatlich hunderte News: neue Wirtshäuser, neue Architekturen, neue Ideen. Nicht alle sind gesund, nicht alle wirklich überlebensfähig, mehrere hart an der Grenze von Genie und Wahnsinn. Das Wichtigste daran ist aber dies: es gibt temperamentvolle Veränderung.

Für jene, die sowas mögen, wurde mit der Copa Cagrana sogar ein Erholungsgebiet an der Donau geschaffen. Dies ist insofern erwähnenswert, als Wien bislang glücklos versuchte, den großen Strom reizvoll zu integrieren – kein Vergleich zur Donau in Budapest, schon gar keiner zur Themse London's oder der Seine von Paris.

Sperrstunde. *Closing time*

The compilers of this book, both the photographer and the writer, existed for a long time in a state of mental derangement. We loved dark Vienna more than anything else. For years we hovered in it like glow worms. As guests of the night we were rather quiet. One of us was often seen with a camera, the other with a fountain pen. We had our fair share of arguments, although we did not get into any fights. At any rate, we we never arrested. All the same, we now know a lot of policemen and several secret service people, those who suspiciously crossed our path of nocturnal industry.

II.

Today, we treat our condition more cautiously. Since then, we have discovered that the early morning is also a good time for creativity. Occasionally, we even pay our respects to country locations. However, we have become neither traitors nor converts. From time to time we still immerse ourselves, though cautiously, in the beauty of that Viennese night which was our love for so long.

"What's seldom is beautiful", say the British. Those excursions which have now become few and far between are especially beautiful. They do not have the inflationary character of that time when we invented the 'daily night'. We have that to thank for minor defeats in our health and great victories in our creative work – or what at first appeared to be so by daylight, and sometimes just burst like a soap-bubble. The overall balance was overwhelmingly positive. We were industrious and excited, thoroughly elated by a genius loci *of the nocturnal old city.*

III.

Of course, the term 'old city' is intended solely in the best sense, as referring to its architectural substance, its historical depth, its great tradition of service architecture, and the serenely muddled interweaving of the green suburbs and the inner city along indistinct internal borders full of surprises.

Apart from these basic values we ought to also talk about a new city. Falter, *that excellent, reliable city magazine, sometimes ruthless and rough in beating up prominent victims, but usually pursuing intelligent justice, records hundreds of 'news' every month: new pubs and restaurants, new buildings, new ideas. Not all of them are healthy, not all of them are capable of survival, some are right on the border between genius and madness. The most important thing, however, is the fact that there is spirited change.*

For those who like such things, a recreation area called the Copa Cagrana was created, up on the Danube. This is worth mentioning insofar as Vienna had for a long time been unsuccessful in its attempts to integrate the great river – there can be no comparison here with the Danube in Budapest, and none at all with the Thames in London or the Seine in Paris.

Die zwei wichtigsten Verbesserungen für den Nachtwanderer haben mit Entbürokratisierung zu tun.

Erstens: Wien ist im Sommer eine Gehsteigstadt geworden. Vieles spielt sich nun vor den Türen im Freien ab. Die Italiener lieben das und kommen in Massen, ein geschmacksicheres Kompliment.

Zweitens: Die Stadtväter killten in ihrer Weisheit den sogenannten Lokalbedarfsparagraphen, der auch staubige Wirte vor Wettbewerb geschützt hatte. So wurde das Bermudadreieck möglich. Modernen Konzeptionisten wie Michael Satke („Reiss", „Roter Engel") waren endlich die Ketten genommen.

IV.

Wer je in Städten wie Lima oder Bogota, aber auch New York und Rom durch die Nachtstadt wanderte, begreift eine wesentliche Begeisterung der Fremden für Wien: ihr Gefühl der Sicherheit.

Sicherheit ist auch den nichtängstlichen Nachtwanderern eine wichtige innere Schönheit. Im Hotel Bristol, keine hundert Meter vom Haupteingang der Wiener Oper entfernt, kennt man glückliche Auslandsgäste. die anfangs nicht glauben mochten, daß man die weite Strecke zur Oper zu Fuß zurücklegen könne, ohne die Perlenkette oder das Leben zu verlieren.

Jedes Bild dieses Buches kann daher furchtlos an der Wirklichkeit überprüft werden.

Wir wünschen den Liebhabern von Wien eine Gute Nacht.

The two most important improvements for the nocturnal wanderer are connected with a reduction of bureaucracy.

Firstly: in summer, Vienna now becomes a city that lives on the pavements. A great many things take place outdoors. The Italians love that and come in their masses, a sure compliment to good taste.

Secondly: the city elders, in their wisdom, have now done away with that section of the law regulating the number of restaurants, which used to protect dusty old pub owners from competition. As a result, the Bermuda Triangle has become a reality. Modern-thinking people with ideas, like Michael Satke (Reiss, Roter Engel) are thus at last free of their fetters.

IV.

Anyone who has ever wandered through cities like Lima, Bogota or, for that matter, New York or Rome, will understand one of the most essential things which helps to fill the foreigner with enthusiasm for Vienna: the feeling of safety.

Safety is also an important inner attraction for night-time wanderers who are not afraid. In Hotel Bristol, less than a hundred metres away from the main entrance to the Vienna Opera, one sees happy foreign visitors who cannot at first believe that it is possible to walk such a great distance to the Opera without losing a pearl necklace or even one's life.

Every picture in this book can therefore be tested against the reality without any fear whatsoever.

We thus wish lovers of Vienna a very good night.

Sperrstundenindex *Index of Closing Times*

CAFES

CAFE CENTRAL, 8-22, So Ruhetag,
1., Herreng. 14, Tel. 5354176
CAFE DRECHSLER, Mo-Fr 4-20, Sa 4-18,
6., Linke Wienzeile 22, Tel. 5878580
CAFE IMPERIAL (im Hotel Imperial), 7-24,
1., Kärntner Ring 16, Tel. 50110-0
CAFE MEIEREI STADTPARK, 10-22 (vom
1.4.-31.10), 3., Heumarkt 2, Tel. 756159
CAFE SACHER (im Hotel Sacher), 7.30-11.30,
1., Philharmonikerstr. 4, Tel. 51456-0
CAFE SIRK (im Hotel Bristol), 10-24, Sommer -23, 1., Kärntner Ring 1, Tel. 51516-0
DIGLAS, 7-23.30, So/Feiertag 10-22.30,
1., Wollzeile 10, Tel. 5128401
DOMCAFE, 10.30-22, 1., Stephansplatz 9,
Tel. 534050
DOMMAYER, 7-24, 13., Dommayerg. 1,
Tel. 825465
EILES, 7-22, Sa/So/Feiertag 8-22,
8., Josefstädter Str. 2, Tel. 423410
FRAUENHUBER, Mo-Fr 8-23, Sa 8-16, So
Ruhetag, 1., Himmelpfortg. 6, Tel. 5124323
GRIENSTEIDL, 8-24, 1., Michaelerplatz 2,
Tel. 5352692
HAAG, 7-22, Sa 8-21, 1., Schotteng. 2,
Tel. 5331810
HAWELKA, Mi-Mo 8-2, So/Feiertag 16-2,
1., Dorotheerg. 6, Tel. 5128230
HUMMEL, 7-2, 8., Josefstädter Str. 66,
Tel. 425314
KLEINES CAFE, 10-2, So/Feiertag 13-2,
1., Franziskanerplatz 3, kein Tel.
KÜNSTLERHAUS NACHTCAFE, 18-4,
1., Karlsplatz 5, Tel. 5053839
LANDTMANN, 8-24, 1., Dr. Karl Lueger-Ring 4,
Tel. 63(533)0621
PRÜCKEL, 9-22, Mo/Mi/Fr/So Klaviermusik
19-22, 1., Stubenring 24, Tel. 5126115
RITTER, 7.30-22, 6., Mariahilfer Str. 73,
Tel. 5878237
SCHWARZENBERG, Konzertcafé, 7-24,
Sa 9-24, 1., Kärntner Ring 17, Tel. 5127393
TIROLERHOF, 7-21, So/Feiertag 9.30-20,
1., Tegetthofstr. 8, Tel. 5127833
WESTEND, 7-23, 7., Mariahilfer Str. 128,
Tel. 933185

HEURIGE/STADTHEURIGE

ALTES PRESSHAUS, 14-24, 19., Cobenzlg.15,
Tel. 322393
BACH-HENGL, 16-24, 19., Sandg. 7-9,
Tel. 3211790
FEUERWEHR-WAGNER, 16-24,
19., Grinzinger Str. 53, Tel. 322442
FUHRGASSL-HUBER, 14.30-24,
19., Neustift a. Walde 68, Tel. 441405
GIGERL, Stadtheuriger, 12-1, Kü -1,
1., Rauhensteing. 3/ Eing. Blumenstockg. 2,
Tel. 5134431
GRINZINGER HAUERMANDL, 17.30-24,
So Ruhetag, 19., Cobenzlg. 20, Tel. 3220444,
323027
HEINRICH NIERSCHER, 15-24, Di/Mi
Ruhetag, 19., Strehlg. 21, Tel. 442146
MAYER AM PFARRPLATZ, 16-24,
19. Heiligenstädter Pfarrplatz 2, Tel. 371287
OPPOLZER, 17-24, So/Feiertag Ruhetag,
19., Himmelstr. 22, Tel. 322416
REINPRECHT, 15.30-24, 19., Cobenzlg. 22,
Tel. 321471
SCHÜBL-AUER, 15.30-24, So Ruhetag,
19., Kahlenberger Str. 22, Tel. 372222
SOWIESO, Stadtheuriger, 17-24,
1., Grashofg.1, Tel. 5126388
URBANI-KELLER, 18-1, 1., Am Hof 12,
Tel. 639102
10ER MARIE, 18-1, So 15.30-22, Mo Ruhetag,
16., Ottakringer Str. 224, Tel. 463116
ZIMMERMANN, 15-24, Sa/So/Feiertag 13-24,
19., Mitterwurzerg. 20, Tel. 441207
ZIMMERMANN, 17-24, So/Feiertag Ruhetag,
19., Armbrusterg. 5, Tel. 372211
ZWÖLF APOSTEL-KELLER, 16.30-24,
1., Sonnenfelsg. 3, Tel. 5126777

RESTAURANTS

BELVEDERESTÖCKL, 12-24 (Sommer),
12-15, 18-24 (Winter), 3., Prinz Eugen-Str. 25,
Tel. 784198
CARPACCIO, Mo-Fr 11-15, 18.30-24, Sa 19-23,
4., Paniglg. 22, Tel. 5059988
DO & CO IM HAASHAUS, Mo-Sa 12-24,
1., Stephansplatz 12, Tel. 5355979
DREI HUSAREN, täglich 12-15, 18-24,
1., Weihburgg. 4, Tel. 5121092
ECKEL, Di-Sa 11.30-14.30, 18-22.30, So/Mo
Ruhetag, Sieveringer Str. 46, Tel. 323218
ELSÄSSER GOURMANDISEN MANUFAKTUR,
Mo-Fr nur gegen Reservierung, 8., Albertg. 19,
Tel. 487067
HAUSWIRTH, Mo-Fr 11.30-15, 18-24,
Sa 18-24, So Ruhetag, 6., Otto Bauer-G. 20,
Tel. 5871261
HEDRICH, Mo-Do 9-21, 1., Stubenring 2,
Tel. 5129588
HUMMERBAR, 18-1, So Ruhetag,
1., Mahlerstr. 9, Tel. 5128843
KORSO, 12-15, 19-1, Sa 19-1, Sommer Sa/So
19-1, 1., Mahlerstr. 2, Tel. 51516-546
PRINZ FERDINAND, Di-So 11-24,
8., Bennoplatz 2, Tel. 4317342
SCHNATTL, Mo-Fr 11.30-14.30, 18-24,
Sa 18-24, 8., Lange G. 40, Tel. 423400
STEINERNE EULE, Di-Sa 11-14.30, 18-1,
7., Halbg. 30, Tel. 932250/937268
STEIRERECK, Mo-Fr 12-14, 19-24, Sa/So/
Feiertag Ruhetag, 3., Rasumovskyg. 2,
Tel. 7133168
VIER JAHRESZEITEN (Hotel Interconti),
12-15, 19-24, Sa Vorm./So Abend geschl.,
3., Johannesg. 28, Tel. 7112203

CHINESISCHE RESTAURANTS

ASIA, täglich 11.30-15, 17.30-24,
1., Himmelpfortgasse 27, Tel. 5127277
BAKAL, Mo-Do 11-15, 17.30-2, Fr-So 11.30-2,
1., Schellingg. 12, Tel. 5134866
GREEN COTTAGE, täglich 12-14.30,
18-23.30, 5., Kettenbrückeng. 3, Tel. 566581
IMPERIAL GARDENS, Mo-Sa 11.30-14.30,
19-23.30, 1., Stubenring 18/Falkestraße,
Tel. 5124911
KIANG, täglich 17-1, 8., Ledererg. 14,
Tel. 423197
LUCKY CHINESE, tägl. 11.30-15, 17.30-24,
1., Kärntnerstr. 24, Tel. 5123428
MING COURT, tägl. 11.30-15, 17.30-1,
1., Kärntnerstr. 32-34, Tel. 5121775
MONGOLISH BARBECUE, tägl. 11.30-14.30,
17.30-0.30, 1., Fleischmarkt 4, Tel. 5353176
ROJER, tägl. 11.30-15, 16.30-24,
1., Eschenbachg. 4, Tel. 564217
RUBIN, tägl. 11.30-15, 17.30-24,
1., Mahlerstr. 9, Tel. 5133901
SHANGHAI, tägl. 12-14.20, 18-24,
1., Jasomirgottstr. 6, Tel. 637419

FRANZÖSISCHE RESTAURANTS

FRANCHI'S, tägl. 11-1, 1., Schwarzenbergpl. 3,
Tel. 7127732
LA BAGUETTE, tägl. 11-24,
1., Rotenturmstr. 12, Tel. 51221
LA CREPERIE, tägl. 11.30-15, 18-24,
1., Jasomirgottstr. 5, Tel. 5335507
SALUT, Mo-Sa 11.30-14, 18-0.30,
1., Wildpretmarkt 3, Tel. 5331322

GRIECHISCHE RESTAURANTS

ACHILLEUS, tägl. 11-15, 17-24,
1., Köllnerhofg. 3, Tel. 5128328
ARTEMIS, Mo 18-23.30, Di-So 11.30-23.30,
1., Griecheng. 3, Tel. 5354169
KOSTAS, tägl. (außer So) 11-24,
1., Friedrichstr. 6, Tel. 563729
ORPHEUS, So-Mi 12-24, Do-Sa 12-2,
1., Spiegelg. 10, Tel. 5123853

INDISCHE RESTAURANTS

KOH-I-NOOR, tägl. 11.30-14.30, 18-23,
1., Marc Aurel Str. 8, Tel. 5330080
MAHARADSCHA, Mo- Fr 17-0.30, Sa, So,
11.30-14.30, 18-23.30, 1., Gölsdorfg. 1,
Tel. 637443

ITALIENISCHE RESTAURANTS

DA CONTE, Mo-Sa 12-15, 18.30-24,
1., Kurrentg. 12, Tel. 5336464
DA BIZI, tägl. 11-24, 1., Rotenturmstr. 4,
Tel. 5133705
GROTTA AZZURRA, Mo-Sa 12-15, 18.30-
23.30, 1., Babenbergerstr. 5, Tel. 5861044
LA NINFEA, Mo-Sa 12-14.30, 18-23.30,
1., Schauflerg. 6, Tel. 5329126
ROSSINI, Mo-Sa 12-14.30, 18.30-23.30,
1., Schönlaterng. 11, Tel. 5126214
SCAMPI, So-Fr 12-15, 18.30-23.30, Sa 18-24,
1., Mahlerstr. 11, Tel. 5132297

JAPANISCHE RESTAURANTS

KO RYO CHUNG, tägl. 12-15, 18-23,
1., Schellingg. 3, Tel. 5121068

SAPPORO INN, tägl. 12-14, 18-23, 3., Heumarkt 9, Tel. 7131199
SUSHI-YU, Mo-Sa 12-14, 18-23, 3., Ungarg. 6, Tel. 7138914
TOKYO, tägl. 12-14, 18-23, 1., Börseg. 3, Tel. 5350392

MEXIKANISCHE RESTAURANTS

MARGARITAVILLE, Mo-Sa 18-2, So 18-24, 1., Bartensteing. 3, Tel. 424786
MEXICANO, Mo-Do 18-24, Fr, Sa bis 1, 1., Rockhgasse 3, Tel. 637516

SPANISCHE RESTAURANTS

EL PULPO, Mo-Sa 18-1, 1., Hafnersteig 8, Tel. 5353071
PUERTO, tägl. 18-2, 1., Rudolfspl. 2, Tel. 5352999

SZENE/BEISLN

ALT-WIEN, 10-2, 1., Bäckerstr. 9, Tel. 525222
APROPOS, 10-2, Sa/So 18-2, 1., Rudolfsplatz 12, Tel. 5334189
ATOLL, 10-2, Mai-September Atoll Beach-Club, Discothek ab 22, 22., Am Segelhafen 2, Tel. 234959
ATRIUM, 20.30-2, Fr/Sa 20-4, 4., Schwarzenbergplatz 10, Tel. 5053594
BETTELSTUDENT, 10-2, Fr/Sa 10-3, 1., Johannesg. 12, Tel. 5132044
BREZELG'WÖLB, 11.30-1, 1., Ledererhof 9, Tel. 638811
CAFE ENGLÄNDER, Mo-Sa 8-1, So/Feiertag 10-1, 1., Postg. 2, Tel. 5122734
CASABLANCA, 18-2, Fr/Sa 18-4, 1., Rabensteig 8, Tel. 5333463
CHAMÄLEON, So-Do 17-2, Fr/Sa 17-4, 1., Blutg. 3, Tel. 5131703
CREPERIE-BRASSERIE SPITTELBERG, 18-24, 7., Spittelbergg. 12, Tel. 961570
DÜSENBERG, 20-3.30, 1., Stubenring 4, Tel. 5138496
ECHO, 12-15, 20-2, Sa 20-2, 1., Passauer Platz 2, Tel. 638984
ENRICO PANIGL, 14-4, Sa/So/Feiertag 19-4, 1., Schönlaterng. 11, Tel. 5151716
EXTRABLATT, 10-4, Sa 19-4, So 19-2, 1., Johannesg. 14, Tel. 5129834
FELLINI, 9-4, Fr/Sa/So 21-5, 1., Seilerstätte 1, Tel. 5131250
FISCHERBRÄU, Erste Wiener Gasthof-Brauerei, 16-1, So 11-1, 19., Billrothstr.17, Tel. 316264
GÖSSER BIERKLINIK, 9-24, Kü -23, So/Feiertag Ruhetag, 1., Steindlg. 4, Tel. 5356897
GRÄFIN VOM NASCHMARKT, 3-2, Mo Ruhetag, 6., Linke Wienzeile 14, Tel. 563389
HOPFERL, 11-21, Sa 11-15, So/Feiertag Ruhetag, 1., Naglerg. 13, Tel. 5332641
HUNGERKÜNSTLER, 19-2, Mo Ruhetag, 6., Gumpendorfer Str. 48, Tel. 5879210
KAKTUS-BAR, 17-2, Fr/Sa 17-4, 1., Seitenstetteng. 5, Tel. 5331938
KITSCH & BITTER, 9-2, Fr/Sa 9-4, 1., Ruprechtsplatz 1, Tel. 5353039

KRAH-KRAH, 11-2, 1., Rabensteig 8, Tel. 6381193
KUCHLDRAGONER, 10-2, So 15-2, 1., Seitenstetteng. 3-5, Tel. 638371
LA CREPERIE, 11.30-14.30/18-24, 1., Jasomirgottstr. 3, Tel. 5335507
LUGECK, 9-24, Sa/So 10-24, 1., Lugeck 7, Tel. 5127979
MILJÖÖ, 10-2, 1., Dorotheerg. 19, Tel. 5131944
MOTTO, 20-4, 5., Schönbrunnerstr. 30, Eingang Rüdigerg., Tel. 5870672
MOZART & MEISL, 17-1, Fr/Sa 17-2, 19., Gymnasiumstr. 62, Tel. 3102097
NEW YORKER, 19-2, Do-Sa 19-4, 1., Biberstr. 9, Tel. 5137529
OSWALD & KALB, 18-1, 1., Bäckerstr. 14, Tel. 5121371/526992
PADRINO, 18-2, So Ruhetag, 1., Schweigg. 3, 5359251
PAPA'S TAPAS, 20-2, Fr/Sa 20-4, täglich Live-Musik, 4., Schwarzenbergplatz 10, Tel. 650311
ROTER ENGEL, Live-Musik, 15-2, Do-Sa 15-4, So 17-2, 1., Rabensteig 5, Tel. 5354105
SALZ & PFEFFER, 19-8, Sa 19-9, 6., Joanellig. 8, Tel. 569277
SALZAMT, 17-4, So 17-2, 1., Ruprechtsplatz 1, Tel. 5333332
STEH-ACHTERL, 19-3, 1., Sterng. 3, Tel. 5336714
WEINMUSEUM, 18-2, Sa 19-2, So/Feiertag Ruhetag, 1., Weihburgg. 18, Tel. 5129702
WEINORGEL, 16-2, 1., Bäckerstr. 2, Tel. 5131227
WIENER, 18-4, 7., Hermanng. 27, Tel. 937228
JAZZLAND, Mo-Sa 19-2, Live-Jazz ab 21, 1., Franz Josefs-Kai 29, Tel. 5332575
JAZZSPELUNKE, 16-2, Sa 11-2, So 14-2, 6., Dürerg. 3, Tel. 5870126
OPUS ONE (Jazzlokal), 20.30-4, 1., Mahlerstr. 11, Tel. 5132075

DISCOS

JACK DANIELS, 21-5, So/Mo/Di 21-4, 1., Krugerstr. 6, Tel. 5124396
MONTEVIDEO, Do-Sa 23-5, 1., Annag. 3a, Tel. 5138574
NACHTWERK, Do-Sa u. vor jedem Feiertag 20-5, 23., Dr. Gondag. 9, Tel. 6168880
P 1, 21-4, Fr 21-6, Sa 20-6, 1., Rotg. 9, Tel. 5359995
QUEEN ANNE, 21-5.30, Mo Live-Musik, 1., Johannesg. 12, Tel. 5120203
TAKE FIVE, 22-5, So/Mo Ruhetag, 1., Annag. 3a, Tel. 5129277
TANZCAFE VOLKSGARTEN, 20-2, Fr/Sa 20-5, So 16-2, Mai-Sept. im Freien, Mo Soul Seduction ab 22, Fr Reggae Night, 1., Volksgarten, Tel 630518
U 4, 23-5, Do Gay-In, 12., Schönbrunnerstr. 222, Tel. 858518
WAKE UP, 21-5, So/Mo/Di 21-4, 1., Seilerstätte 5, Tel. 5122112

WÜRSTELSTÄNDE

ALBERTINA, Ecke Operng./Goetheg., täglich bis 2
ASPERNBRÜCKE, bei der Urania, Mo-Fr 8-4, So 16-4
BURGRING 5, Staßenbahnhaltestelle Babenbergerstraße, vor dem Kunsthistorischen Museum
HOHER MARKT, täglich 9-2
DR. KARL LUEGER-RING, „Würstel Richard", bei Straßenbahnhaltestelle Schottentor, Mo-Fr 8-1, Sa 10-1, So 13-1
NUSSDORFERSTRASSE 79, Ecke Währinger Gürtel, täglich 7-4
DR. KARL RENNER-RING, Kiosk, Bellaria Buffet, bei Endstelle von Linie 46 & 49, Mo-Fr 7-12

BARS

AMERICAN-BAR (LOOS-BAR), 18-4, 1., Kärntner Str. 10, Tel. 512 32 83
BANE, Café-Bar, 11-4, Sa/So/Feiertag 19-4, 1., Köllnerhofg. 3, Tel. 5120279
BONBONNIERE, 15-2, So Ruhetag, 1., Spiegelg. 15, Tel. 5126886
BORA-BORA, 17-4, Do/Fr/Sa 17-5, 1., Johannesg. 12, Tel. 5122784
BRISTOL BAR (im Hotel Bristol), 11-1, August 15.30-1, 1., Kärnter Ring 1, Tel. 51516-0
BROADWAY PIANO-BAR, Mo-Sa ab 21, So Ruhetag, 1., Bauernmarkt 21, Tel. 5332849
CHATTANOOGA, 8-3, Fr/Sa 8-4, 1., Graben 29a, Tel. 5335000
CONTE-BAR, 9-4, 1., Elisabethstr. 1, Tel. 5874727
ECHO-BAR, 11.30-15, 20-2, Sa 20-2, So Ruhetag, 1., Passauer Platz 2, Tel. 638984
EDEN-BAR, 22-4, 1., Lilieng. 2, Tel. 5127450
GALERIE BAR, Mo-Sa 19-4, 1., Singerstr. 7, Tel. 5124929
JOSEPHINE, Bar des offiziellen Innenstadt-Bordells, Mo-Fr 11-4, Sa/So 20-4, 1., Sonnenfelsg. 9, Tel. 5129369
MAPITOM-BAR, So-Do 17.30-1, Fr/Sa 17.30-2, 1., Seitenstetteng. 5, Tel. 5354513
MARC AUREL, 20-3, So Ruhetag, 3., Landstraßer Hauptstr. 38, Tel. 730831
MARIA THERESIA BAR (im Hotel Imperial), 16-24, 1., Kärntner Ring 16, Tel. 50110-0
MAXIM, 12-5, 1., Opernring 11, Tel. 563340
MOULIN ROUGE, 22-6, Programm 23-ca. 1.30: Artistik, Striptease, Magie, Tanz; Sommer So Discothek, 1., Walfischg. 11, Tel. 5122130
REISS-BAR, Champagnertreff, 11-3, Sa 10-3, 1., Marco-D'Aviano-G. 1, Tel. 5127198
ROTE BAR (im Hotel Sacher), 12-1, 1., Philharmonikerstr. 4, Tel. 51456-0
SEINERZEIT, Tanzbar, Di-So 20-2, 6., Wallg. 16/Ecke Strohmayerg., Tel. 5978345
SPLENDID, 22-4, 1., Jasomirgottstr. 3, Tel. 5353430
STAMPERL, 11-2, Sa/So 17-4, 1., Steing. 1, Tel. 5336250